Chicago Schools: 'Worst in America'

*An examination
of the public schools
that fail Chicago*

Chicago Schools: 'Worst in America'

*An examination
of the public schools
that fail Chicago*

By the staff of the
Chicago Tribune

Chicago Tribune

Chicago Tribune photos by Ovie Carter
except where indicated

Published by The Chicago Tribune
435 North Michigan Ave., Chicago, Ill. 60611
Manufactured in the United States of America
International standard book number: 0-9621267-0-5

Printing courtesy of R. R. Donnelley & Sons Company
Chicago

*To the children
of Chicago Public Schools*

Contents

Preface

This is a reprint of a tragic story. A story that says the Chicago public school system is so bad that nothing short of wiping it out and starting over can save public education in one of the nation's great cities.

The conclusion is hard to accept. But drawing it was easy. In a seven month examination of what experts have called the "worst public schools in America," Chicago Tribune reporters found overwhelming, damning evidence that the experts were right.

With a few notable exceptions, Chicago schools are failing miserably the dual mission of preparing young people to realize the dreams that are their birthright and of providing for the city's future a qualified and productive citizenry.

The report from Goudy Elementary School classrooms, which are representative of the system, was stark and poignant. Such schools, it showed, are hardly more than daytime warehouses for inferior students, taught by disillusioned and inadequate teachers, presided over by a bloated, leaderless bureaucracy, and constantly undercut by a selfish, single-minded teachers' union that has somehow captured and intimidated the political power structure of both city and state governments.

The outlook for improvement is not hopeful, the reporting showed, mainly because public schools students in Chicago are increasingly the children of the poor, the black and the Hispanic—a constituency without a champion in the corridors of executive and legislative power. To many politicians, public school systems such as Chicago's are a symbol of urban decay beyond help, a bottomless pit of incompetence and a waste of both tax dollars and political capital.

But the condition of Chicago's public schools, as documented in this series of stories in May, 1988, is simply another chapter in a larger story that The Tribune has been reporting in depth since 1983—the impact on society of the new underclass that has taken root and become permanent in America.

The sorry state of these schools today is but a manifestation within the institution of public education of yesterday's mistakes, an expensive result of the political orphaning of the urban poor during the last two decades.

The despair that marks the daily experiences of students and teachers in the public schools is symptomatic of their lives, as detailed in two previous Tribune series, The American Millstone, in 1985, and The Chicago Wall in 1986.

Perhaps more tragically, it portends an ominous future, not only for them and their children but for the rest of us.

It took an extraordinary combination of greed, racism, political cowardice and public apathy to let the public schools in Chicago get so bad off. It will take an extraordinary combination of public education and political courage to fix them again.

Unless we understand what happened and react courageously, the same cycle of deprivation and dependency will continue to encircle an increasingly large segment of America. And this underclass will continue to be a millstone on the society, impacting public institutions to a degree way out of proportion to its size, the way it did the Chicago schools.

James D. Squires
Editor
Chicago Tribune

Rare moment: *A Goudy student receives some personal instruction in a school where, despite a teachers union contract calling for smaller class sizes, as many as 39 energetic children are assigned to one teacher.*

Welcome to Goudy school, where the future dies early

Is the student breathing?
'Yes.' 'Then no report.'

Principal Thomas J. "Doc" McDonald reaches up to smooth a shock of white hair that has spilled onto his forehead. He notices the smudge of blood on his hand. Then he lunges, eyes flashing. *"Give me that pipe!"*

Circling him in the second-floor hallway are two pre-teen students, Arnaray Bibbs, who is armed with a long, unraveled piece of cardboard tubing, and Maurice Elliston, who is swinging a stubby piece of copper pipe.

No one wants to hurt anybody. It is a game, actually, not uncommon in this schoolhouse. To see who can last the longest.

To see who will flinch.

"Give me that pipe," McDonald tells Maurice, turning his back on Arnaray, who swings the cardboard tubing and whacks the principal on the backside. McDonald spins around to deal with Arnaray and then Maurice jabs the pipe at his behind. The hair bobs as he pivots. His face burns red. *"I said give me that damned pipe!"*

" Shut up, Doc," says Maurice, who has abruptly tired of this exercise. He flings the pipe weakly. McDonald grabs it.

But no one really wins.

Welcome to Goudy Elementary, a place where children with no other options for an education are learning their first and probably their most important lessons about school.

It is hardly the best of what Chicago Public Schools have to offer.

It is far from the worst.

It is one of the 402 regular elementary schools run by a school system that U.S. Secretary of Education William Bennett has called the worst in the nation. A seven-month Tribune examination has found that whether the system is the worst or not, it is a disgrace.

Behind the walls of this hollow educational warehouse at 5120 N. Winthrop Ave., the futures of 690 children from the Uptown neighborhood are being silently but certainly shaped by an antiquated system where education is often secondary to a maze of other interests and where each day is a test of endurance in which the most important lesson to be learned by anyone is how to survive the 5½-hour school day.

"I call this the William C. Goudy Non-Academy," McDonald says as he tends to the wound on his finger.

"It's a gravity school. I take anything that walks in."

The brick is sallow, tired-looking. Painted window frames have peeled. What passes for a play area around this rectangular, three-story fortress is a forbidding expanse of buckling pavement that spills into a back alley without the benefit of a protective fence.

There is no recess.

There are no swings. Not even a rusted jungle gym. Just the lonely poles that support three graffiti-scarred backboards stripped of all but one bent basketball rim.

Sometimes the morning bell rings at 9 precisely. Sometimes, at 9:05. Usually, school begins whenever somebody in the office remembers to push the button. The automated bell ringing system installed a year ago by the Board of Education has been serviced once, but it has not rung automatically yet.

"Let's go! Let's go!" barks Maria Bonilla, a hallway monitor who is one of the first faces to greet the children each morning, frowning as she uses her whole arm to wave the sea of incoming bodies toward two sets of stairs.

Not five minutes pass and into the main school office walks teacher Fani Cahill with the first of this day's casualties. She has her arm around Frank Kotszycki, who is still wearing a milk mustache from his breakfast and who has a big red bump above his left ear.

"Ms. Trigg," begins Cahill, trying to snag the attention of the school clerk, who has a way of making it clear that she does not like to be bothered. "Frank refused to go into the room this morning, again, and there was a scuffle with the security guard and his head was banged up against the lockers."

"There is a bump," Cahill says, pulling the 12-year-old over so that she can run her fingers over the swollen spot. "Do I need to fill out an accident report?"

"Is he breathin'?" Vera Trigg asks without looking up from her newspaper.

"Yes, I'm afraid he is," Cahill admits.

"Then no report."

Beyond the high-profile magnet schools and special programs that lure children from the most motivated families on the promise of something better sit the schools for 73 percent of the 419,537 children who are enrolled in Chicago Public Schools. They are the children who have been left behind.

Goudy is one of the regular neighborhood schools festering in academic and spiritual distress.

In Chicago, nearly half of the children who enter the public school system drop out before graduating from high school. The underpinnings of this failure begin early in elementary school, the years when a child may be turned on to the idea of an education or forever lost.

As part of its examination of the schools, The Tribune spent nearly four months inside Goudy Elementary to see what public education has come to mean.

There is nothing selective about a school like Goudy. Its doors are open to anyone—not only all the children who happen to live in the neighborhood, but also to all teachers the system assigns, no matter what their ability or expertise.

Some children who go to school here come from stable homes. Some are reared in families where one or both parents work. But almost all of the children who depend on this school for a grounding in basic academic and behavioral skills are like 68 percent of the children in the city's public schools: They are poor.

Goudy's students emerge from the corridor of unrelenting poverty that cuts through the northern fringe of Uptown, a depressed pocket on the North Side where welfare is the going wage.

Though the school sits in a census area where only about 50 percent of the residents have been tallied as low-income, 98 percent of the Goudy students come from families so poor that the children qualify for the federal government's free lunch.

Like many neighborhood schools in poor communities, Goudy serves a population so transient that about half of the students who arrive in the fall are gone before June. New students arrive continually to take their place.

As is the case throughout the public school system, the students at Goudy are overwhelmingly minority: 45.1 per-

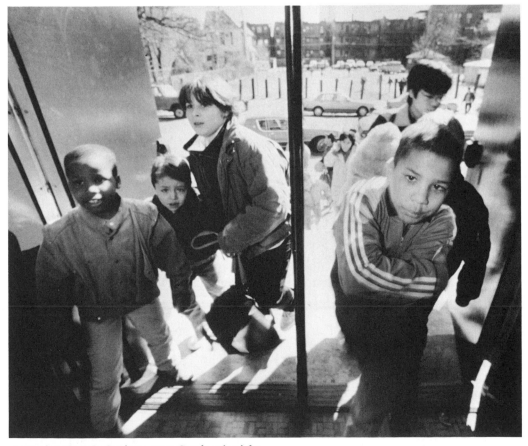

Answering the bell: *Students enter Goudy school for another day. "It's a gravity school. I take anything that walks in," says Principal Thomas McDonald.*

cent are Hispanic, 34.3 percent are black, 11.2 percent are Asian and 2 percent are American Indian; 7.4 percent are white.

To walk with these children, to follow in their footsteps, is to take a journey through a world where everything is not always what it seems.

It is a place where the principal is also a truant officer and social worker because the system has not provided enough of that kind of support. The building engineer, at $34,301 a year, makes more than many teachers.

Because of a professed lack of space, some children attend reading class for the better part of the school year in a noisy auditorium. Others get their lessons in the school's garage-like annex, seated at desks shoved together in a narrow hall. Two remedial classes of 1st graders, many of whom have already flunked a year, share one confusing classroom where bulletin boards serve as a makeshift and hardly soundproof divider between the groups.

But children are often secondary to other considerations when it comes to doling out the rooms.

Except for the small reading group she teaches each morning, Susan Malis, a teacher with political clout, has an entire classroom virtually to herself. It is her office. Complete with a telephone.

Audrey Wilborn, the school's first full-time librarian in four years, was amazed to find books were covered with dust and spilling into haphazard piles on the floor.

"Library was free time and a break for the teacher," Wilborn observed as she wrestled a pencil from a 2d grader who had scribbled over the words of Dr. Seuss.

"It had nothing to do with learning to appreciate a book."

Though the two 8th-grade classrooms are side by side, the teachers seldom share their plans. Still smarting from political battles about who would get to teach the most motivated students, they do not always speak.

In the history book used by the brighter class of 8th graders, Ronald Reagan is president. The slower class reads from a text in which Richard M. Nixon is still in office.

All kinds of "lessons" are taught at Goudy.

Children are entrusted with flag duty at some schools as a way of teaching responsibility and civic pride. At Goudy, it is the responsibility of building engineer Dennis McGovern and his staff of five janitors.

After school one Friday, one of McGovern's men did not tend the American flag. It was left flapping at top of the pole. By Saturday, it was lying in a crumpled heap on the muddy ground where it was pelted by a fierce spring rain.

By Sunday morning, it was stolen.

Up in Room 303, where the federal government is spending nearly $75,000 so students can receive remedial instruction in reading and math, teacher Ruby Smith, who aspires to be a principal, explains that she does not actually "teach" because her elaborate computer system tells children how to chart their own course of study in her room.

Smith is paid $34,110 a year and has enough of a budget to pay for a full-time aide to help her with the six groups of 16 children who come to her room, a luxury the system does not provide for regular classroom teachers who are responsible for as many as 39 children at one time.

By the end of this school year, a little more than $1 million will have been invested in the repair of this building to ensure that public education will continue for maybe another 51 years in honor of William C. Goudy, an Illinois statesman who in the 1800s established a reputation as a brilliant courtroom attorney and for whom this school was named.

One afternoon, 8th-grader Marc Venton began to chuckle as he watched a laborer on his hands and knees replacing the black and maroon checkerboard squares of floor tile with light-colored tiles that make the hallways look brighter but will certainly show dirt.

"What a joke," Venton said.

"It's like when your mom tells you to clean up your room and you put all your dirty clothes in a closet.

"That's not going to make this a good school."

'W ould Earl Davis please report to the office. If you are in the building, please come to the office. You should now be in reading. Thank you."

There is a M*A*S*H-like atmosphere about Goudy. All day long, voices crackle over the public address system. The principal interrupts one afternoon to alert the whole school that a group of boys is running wild in the second-floor corridor. The clerk sends her voice into classrooms when she needs to know something, when she wants to continue an argument after a teacher has stormed out of the office, or on paydays when she orders some teachers to come to the office

during classtime to pick up their "negotiables," the school's euphemism for paychecks. The word has been used ever since a teacher said she complained that she did not feel secure when the word "paychecks" was announced in the presence of the low-income students who attend Goudy.

Assistant principal Paul Goldstein sends out all-points-bulletins for students who walk to their morning reading class and keep on walking, right out of the school.

On this day, Earl and a classmate walked down Foster Avenue to the McDonald's.

"We stayed there until reading was over," Earl, who is 13, explained the next day. "Reading is horrible. Boring. The same old thing day after day, story after story in this dumb book.

"You just want to escape sometimes. There's nothing to do in this school that's fun."

Children cry out for something more.

But they do not get it at this neighborhood school.

There is no science lab. No art teacher. The school is rich in remedial programs that draw attention to a child's failures. But there are no real extra-curricular activities that might help children excel in something either before or after the school day.

Two pianos shoved up against a wall in the auditorium served as bookshelves for a reading teacher for much of the year. At least they are good for something since there is no music program any more.

There is no Parent Teacher Association. No student council. Not a single notebook, T-shirt, or pencil that has been stamped with the school's name.

There used to be a pretty good basketball team called the "Goudy Cougars." But the team is history. So are all the trophies. Years ago, they were stolen.

Organized team activities come on a good day in gym class that takes place on a hardwood floor that begs for a good varnishing and under huge windows protected by steel mesh and framed by heavy mustard-colored curtains that hang in shreds.

Though private washrooms reserved for the principal and the teachers are

Today's lesson: *Teacher Fani Cahill and Principal Thomas McDonald escort a student to the office after a spitting incident. "I think to myself: 'My God, what's happening to all these kids?'" says a 19-year Goudy veteran.*

kept in good supply, soap, paper toweling and toilet paper are not always available for the children. For the better part of the school year, there wasn't even a working toilet paper dispenser for the boys. The school was cut down to only two working washrooms for 690 children to accommodate the contractor's renovation schedule. By Thursdays, the entire second floor would be permeated by the smell of the boys' washroom. On Fridays, the odor would be gone.

Up until this year, teachers were allowed to walk their classes a few blocks to the public library for an enrichment period. But the district office put a stop to that after an assailant ripped a gold chain off teacher Mary Terretta's neck on the sidewalk, right in front of her students.

New to Goudy this year are the two long rows of Apple computers in Dan Griffin's classroom. Paid for by the federal government, this is where the older children learn word processing and computer programming, and it is one of the few rooms in the building where the children do not bolt toward the door when the class is over.

But this may be short-lived. The program is now in jeopardy because Goudy was informed that the money may not be available next year.

Aside from what happens in the classrooms between 9 a.m. and 2:30 p.m., about the only other activity for students at Goudy is eating. Even that is not all fun.

Though the building is being renovated, there are no plans for a lunchroom. The school was built without one in 1937 when the neighborhood was different and when school officials felt they could safely send the children home to eat and then trust them to return.

So some children use a first-floor classroom that is a makeshift eating area. It is small. Stuffy. A tragicomic theater when tempers flare.

"Stand back! Stand back!" warned lunchroom attendant Richard James, who one day in a moment of desperation grabbed a wooden spatula and swatted it at 13-year-old Berlington Card, who, to the delight of his lunchroom audience, was acting his usual role of trying to make James crazy, this time by trying to touch all the onion rings in an aluminum pan.

Most children, however, dine in the school auditorium, where awkward hands must negotiate food trays down long aisles and then carefully balance them on laps, portable lunch tables or adjustable desktops while sitting in hard, splintery chairs. A janitor usually positions himself near the stage with a mop and bucket to tend to the inevitable mess from spilled trays.

Even when well-meaning teachers try to get activities going for the benefit of the children, their colleagues often greet them with a cold response.

Librarian Wilborn sent a note around to all of the teachers one day asking if they would take part in a special "Goudy School Ethnic Fair" that she wanted to plan.

"These teachers make me sick," Fani Cahill sighed as she read over the list, on which 7 of 16 teachers had responded with "no" by the time the sheet arrived in her room.

"Every time you want to do something for school spirit, they say they don't have any time," Cahill complained. "Well, what do they have

time for?"

Then she gave her middle desk drawer a ferocious yank and rummaged until she found a sharpened pencil.

"Yes," Cahill scribbled onto the paper. *"Of course."*

There is one extra-curricular activity of sorts during the schoolday.

It's called "playleading."

"I'm going to tell on you all, I mean it," yells Mark Brown, a skinny 8th grader whose arms are flailing as he tries to corral the tiny kids scampering in all directions as they run out of the washroom. It was his job to manage their bathroom recess.

In the kindergarten room, 8th-grader Tracy Logan is frowning as she wipes off desktops and cleans up after children who have left crumbs from their cheeseburger lunch.

"It's all right, I guess," Tracy says, shrugging when asked about her task.

Seventh-grader Wanda Jackson slams the door to Room 312 behind her. She glowers at the 3d graders who are laughing as they run around the room. Her shoulders visibly stiffen.

"I hate this," she snarls, a menacing look on her face. "I hate little kids."

"Playleading" is another Goudy euphemism. It is the time every day when older students are pulled away from their studies to tend to children so the teachers can take their union-negotiated breaks.

'Keisha, look at me. Look at me! I said look me in the eye. Did you hear me? Look at me, Keisha!"

Counselor Barbara Boxton was livid. Sitting in front of her in the counseling office was 6th-grader LaKeisha

Showers, a girl who only last year was attending Goudy in dresses but who had been coming to school in blue jeans and boys' black gym shoes.

Now, Boxton was trying to make sense out of a situation where LaKeisha beat up classmate Danny Beals in an argument over a brown crayon.

This was not the LaKeisha that Boxton knew.

When she taught 4th grade and La-Keisha was one of her students, the girl made an impression as a polite child whose behavior was as feminine as the pretty dresses she liked to wear.

But a lot can happen in two years.

"Why in the world would you go after a boy like that?" Boxton was saying. "I am so disappointed in you. Look at me, Keisha! You *know* I care about you. You told me I was your favorite teacher, isn't that what you said?"

"You was until today," LaKeisha whispered, turning her head ever so slowly and, when she finally looked directly at Boxton, the tears spilled out of her eyes.

Boxton watched her and slumped a little in her chair. Then she exhaled, and the sound filled the office.

"We're losing her," she said as she watched LaKeisha's tears drip onto a page in her math book. "I'm just watching her slip away.

Final year: *8th graders ham it up at Goudy, where 70% of last year's graduates scored below norms on reading tests.*

"I don't know what's going on in that room."

School cannot be all things to all children, particularly for those who may need the most. There is only so much of a connection that a school counselor like Boxton can make through tough talk and a little intervention.

Fights were common among the children assigned to Room 305. One day it was LaKeisha and Danny. Another day it was Larry Brantley who, in an argument over one of those "he say, she say" things, punched a girl so hard that he was sent to the principal's office and she was given a wet piece of paper toweling to reduce the size of the welt.

Their teacher, Susan Belter, was the first to admit that something was terribly wrong.

"I have a room of 39 overage, unmotivated 6th and 7th graders," explained Belter. "Most of them have already flunked one year of school.

"And I am not prepared for this. I have absolutely no idea of what to do."

Because the neediest children in the upper elementary grades can be the most difficult to motivate, these students often become educational hot potatoes when it comes to assigning children to teachers.

Although Belter, a former welfare caseworker who is a full-time substitute teacher, has been praised for past accomplishments, she was given a roomful of the school's abysmal achievers in her third year at Goudy.

No one suggested that Belter might excel with a group of older students at risk of turning off on school.

Susan Malis, a teacher who also does administrative chores, said Belter got the assignment because it was good for

teachers' morale to pass such groups around.

"It was my turn," Belter said.

During the first half of the school year, one of Belter's students threatened suicide. One ran away from home and a second talked about doing the same. Two are children of neighborhood prostitutes.

In March, after episodes including a near physical attack from a parent when Belter gave a child an F, Principal McDonald removed her from her full-time teaching post.

And when she left Room 305, it was with the sinking feeling that while she had tried to help her needy students, she had actually spent a lot of time pushing them out the door.

One day, in the middle of a lesson, one of her students just got up and left. That in itself was not unusual. But when he came back, he was sweaty and laughing. Then he was summoned out of the room.

"He just walked out of the school, walked to Broadway, stole a woman's purse, and the woman chased him all the way into the school to get it back," Belter explained.

"And he thought it was funny."

Dorothy Nygren had to do a little detective work to get the Apple computer into her classroom.

When she spotted the abandoned machine in the schoolhouse one day, she found out that it had been assigned to a teacher who no longer wanted it.

Public school teachers are often good scavengers. They have to be when all the Board of Education provides for instructional materials beyond the basics like books, paste and paper is $28 per teacher for the entire school year.

In her classroom, Nygren leads her students on pretend archeological digs. She teaches ballet and uses chalkboard trays as the barre. On Fridays, there are enough musical instruments so each child can participate in rhythm band.

Not every teacher has Nygren's creativity and energy.

And few have the extra $500 she received this year to provide for a lot of the "extras"—like the the special art supplies and the oversized word-and-picture books on mythology—that the 36 children who have been grouped together as the brightest of the school's 3d and 4th graders use in her room.

Nygren and three other teachers at Goudy receive this money as part of the state-funded "gifted" program in the regular neighborhood schools. The term "gifted" is usually a misnomer because although some testing is involved, the standards for acceptance vary with the neighborhood and the school. Generally, these children tend to be the most motivated children left after the city magnet schools skim off the best.

When Goudy's fourth such classroom opened this year for 6th and 7th graders, McDonald said he couldn't even bribe some of his teachers to take the room because of the extra work.

So he said he settled for a teacher who came to Goudy on an administrative transfer after being suspended for three days on a charge of striking a child at another school. The teacher, Helen Manos, maintains it was an accident.

Only 15 to 20 percent of Goudy's students land in these so-called gifted classrooms.

The majority of the children are placed in the regular classrooms, where they are so far behind that even the most generous estimate by McDonald suggested that only about 25 percent of them are performing at grade level.

These children learn their lessons in rooms where, despite the union contract calling for lower limits, as many as 39 energetic children are assigned to one teacher.

Fourth-grade teacher David LaRue is short 12 English books and 10 science books for his 37 students.

Henry Caldwell has no real geography books. He improvises, partly with the benefit of scenes of America depicted on the calendars he has hung over the chalkboards.

First-grade teacher Helen Harris has been asking to have writing lines painted on her chalkboard since 1964.

Ann Jardine, who teaches a remedial class of 1st graders, was amazed to see the difference when she dipped into her own pocket and spent $80 to replace the tattered reading books she had.

"You can see it in their eyes," Jardine said. "And by the way they touch them. They don't even realize they're developing a love for a book."

In January, not even midway through the school year, clerk Vera Trigg had to begin rationing pencils, construction paper, paper clips, writing paper and other supplies. She had watched in disbelief one day as her funds for instructional supplies were slashed from $1,504.76 to $13.76. The cutback was part of Goudy's contribution to the money that the school board cut from other parts of its budget to scrape up a raise to settle this year's record teachers' strike.

The most basic of supports for the classroom teacher are lacking as well.

The title of school social worker is actually a misnomer for Edna McCoy, who explained that the personal counseling she would like to offer the children was virtually impossible because the budget cuts trimmed her visits from once a week to twice a month.

The same round of cutbacks also meant that truant officer James Ellis reports to Goudy once a week instead of twice.

Dedicated teachers cry out for something better.

"I want to be a part of something I believe in," said teacher Nancy Banks, who has taught at Goudy all but one of her 33 years in the public schools.

When she was younger, she did things like visit homes and try to provide a social connection for her needy students. Sometimes, she even invited students to visit her house. But so many children with so many needs simply became too much.

"You try," said Banks. "If you care, you always try. But I am constantly amazed by how little I am able to do."

In 1978, back when Banks had more than just a glimmer of hope about the future of the public schools, she bought the manual and studied and took the exam to qualify her to be a principal.

"I really thought I could make a difference," Banks said.

Two years passed without the results being posted. Finally, she received a letter from the Board of Examiners explaining that because of funding constraints and declining student enrollment, the system had no need for more principals and was simply tossing the exam out.

Banks keeps the letter in its original envelope.

In detached bureaucratic language, it wished Banks, anonymously referred to as a principal "candidate," continued success in her professional career.

It makes no mention of how she performed on the test.

"Couldn't they at least have told me if I passed?" she asked.

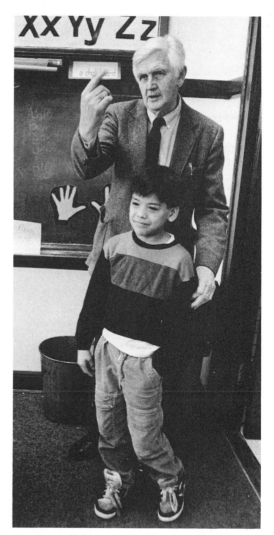

On the prowl: *Thomas "Doc" McDonald stops in a bilingual class to advise the kids. The principal also serves as truant officer and social worker.*

A long time ago, Principal McDonald found his own formula. During his 39 years with the public schools, he has mastered the most important lesson to be learned by anyone: How to get by.

Politics? He knows how to play that game.

"Oh, I'm very nice to Susan Malis," he explained, unabashedly admitting that he has benefitted greatly by having Malis on his staff.

"I give her a nice room. She's brought a lot of money into this school."

Malis is the daughter of Louise Malis, a former Chicago PTA president who during the 1960s and '70s rose to prominence as an influential member of the Board of Education.

McDonald, who is 65 and has been principal of Goudy for 20 years, said he believes it was the presence of Malis that provided him with the clout to attract major reading enrichment programs to Goudy, which was selected from among many public schools where the students had abysmally low reading scores.

For six years, Malis has held what is now a $32,563-a-year position as one of Goudy's two special reading teachers.

Though Malis acknowledges what she called "real problems" with the kind of instruction offered in some of the school's reading classes, she said she rarely ventures into classrooms to assist or offer much teaching advice even though those duties are within her purview.

Instead, she explained, she spends a lot of her time coordinating reading materials and doing administrative work for the principal.

So at Goudy, where 70 percent of last year's 8th-grade class scored below national norms on reading tests, the special reading resource teacher devotes a lot of time to programming the school day, organizing class rosters, tabulating promotion and failure reports, ordering textbooks, conducting standardized tests, serving as a liaison with the renovation contractors, and raising money to make up for funding cuts by organizing the events in which children sell gift items, candy and taffy apples.

It's all a matter of priorities, McDonald likes to explain.

'My mother said it was the opportunity of a lifetime," 9-year-old Twanna Walker said of her decision to leave Goudy in the first semester to attend a special academic program at Pritzker Elementary School on the Near Northwest Side.

Twanna still walks through the alley and across Winthrop Avenue to Goudy every morning, but more than an hour earlier than she did before. One in a cavalcade of yellow schoolbuses picks her up and takes her on a trip that can be as long as an hour, door to door.

But even the best of what the public school system has to offer is imperfect.

Sometimes the buses are late. Or they just do not come.

Which is one reason 12-year-old Uday Khedkar is back at Goudy.

For most of the year, Uday stationed himself outside of Goudy as early as 7:30 so he wouldn't miss his ride to 7th grade at Whitney Young Magnet School on the West Side.

"I really liked it," Uday explained.

"But it was just too hard to get there. The buses either didn't come or I missed some school because they were late. I took the train for a while, but that was very difficult. I had to transfer. My dad tried to get me in a better school that was closer, but the programs were all full."

So in May, Uday transferred back to Goudy, his neighborhood school.

At Whitney Young, he said, he could put his hands on flasks and beakers in a laboratory instead of reading about science in an outdated textbook. He had a laminated student identification card that he proudly snapped onto his shirt. He could sit in a real lunchroom and comfortably eat his lunch.

His English class was for high school credit, and one of his last assignments was to write a sonnet.

In the "gifted" classroom at Goudy, Uday said that the biggest academic challenge he has had during the 90 minutes assigned to reading and English each morning is an assignment on sentence forms.

"It's really boring," said Uday. "The work is so much easier and I spend most of my time just sitting around. I usually finish quicker than the other kids, so I just do all of my homework in class.

"It's really depressing to be back in this school."

Well-meaning teachers find that they have to wrestle with a lot more than academic standards if they hope to make education more than an abstraction.

Children know to go to Room 304 if they need a sweater for winter or maybe a nice pair of jeans. Eighth-grade teacher Bernice Eiland keeps bags of donated clothing for them in the back of her room.

Before she took a personal leave, children would stream into Room 306 all day long to see teacher Fani Cahill. Some wanted to borrow one of the special reading books Cahill kept in her closet. Others simply sought her. Cahill did not know the Cambodian girl who was standing shyly outside her classroom one day two years ago. The 6th grader was pregnant, and Cahill was the one to whom she confided.

Though it may not always stand out as a beacon of hope in a tired neighborhood, the schoolhouse is often the closest thing to stability that many of its families know.

Teacher Helen Harris discovered this before school one morning when she looked up and saw a young mother standing at her door.

"She said, 'I just killed my baby, Mrs. Harris. What should I do?' " Harris remembered. "It happened many years ago, but it really made an impression on me. She came here because this building was the only consistent thing in her life."

Failing disadvantaged students for lack of achievement is discouraged at Goudy. In the long run, Principal McDonald believes, failure in the early years may not be the best solution for the underachieving child.

So each year, often regardless of what a lot of them have accomplished, hundreds of children are promoted after receiving what often amounts to a passive exposure to learning, a concept that is troubling to teachers who recognize that the future is being shaped a little bit with the passing of each school day.

"We're just pushing them through, pushing them through," observed

LaRue, the 4th-grade teacher. "It just scares me to death."

Every year, teacher Dan Griffin attends the graduation ceremony at Senn Metropolitan Academy, the neighborhood high school where most of Goudy's graduates enroll.

"I know a lot of them move out of the neighborhood," said Griffin, who has taught at Goudy for 19 years. "But every year I look at the program that lists all the graduating seniors and I just don't see the names I should be seeing.

"And I think to myself: 'My God, what's happening to all these kids?' "

Lunch-hour shuffle: *The auditorium serves as a lunchroom at Goudy, where little hands negotiate trays down long aisles and laps become tabletops.*

Goudy has been fraught with potential safety hazards this year during rehabilitation. One Friday, as Principal McDonald was making his afternoon rounds, he noticed that one of the two stairways was still blocked off by painters who stood on scaffoldings and rolled a thin coat of dull, beige paint over the walls.

McDonald was afraid that children might get hurt.

He walked briskly to his office, rolled his chair over close to the microphone and sent a message over the intercom into each classroom.

"Teachers. We have a safety problem. The painters are still working on the north stairway. It is blocked off and a very dangerous situation, so please walk your children out of the building and out to the sidewalk to ensure their safety. Again, teachers, walk your children to the sidewalk. Please."

McDonald swung his chair away, folded up his half-glasses, and tucked them into his jacket pocket.

"They won't do it," he said.

Several minutes before the bell was rung, 25-year-veteran teacher Bette Jarrow was the first to bound down the stairs and race toward the office, without her students, to sign out for the day.

Close behind, and laughing with Jarrow as the two scurried down the main corridor, was Rudolph Gonzalez, a substitute whose 4th-grade room was in such an uproar that day that both the assistant principal and McDonald had come in to help him establish order. On one visit, McDonald found Gonzalez with his back literally pinned against the wall by a group of laughing boys.

Children started to run down the one available staircase, the older ones leading the charge.

"Go home!" yelled hallway monitor Maria Bonilla, frowning as she gestured madly toward the school's south door. "This door! Go home! Go home!"

Reading teacher Nanette Turetgen had a wild look about her as she obediently tried to hold a group of young children behind her outstretched arms at the bottom of the staircase. A bewildered Mary Leahu came down the steps looking for her 3d-grade students. But they had already fled.

When the bell finally rang, McDonald walked over to a window at the back of the school office. He pushed back the curtain and took inventory of the teachers who had done what he had asked.

Of the 34 teachers assigned to Goudy, he was able to count those he spotted on the sidewalk on one hand.

"It doesn't surprise me," McDonald said, shrugging.

"You get used to it.

"You see, when you've been here as long as I have, you come to realize that not a lot of what goes on in this building happens for the benefit of the kids."

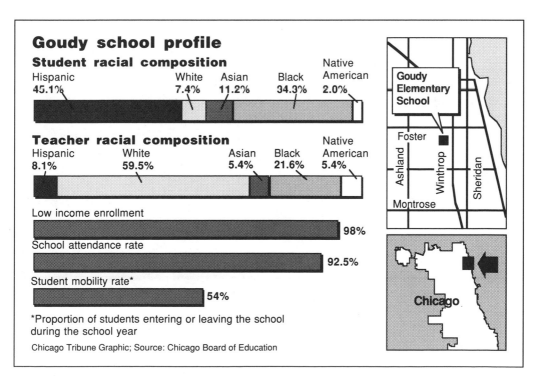

Goudy school profile

Student racial composition

Hispanic	White	Asian	Black	Native American
45.1%	7.4%	11.2%	34.3%	2.0%

Teacher racial composition

Hispanic	White	Asian	Black	Native American
8.1%	59.5%	5.4%	21.6%	5.4%

Low income enrollment 98%
School attendance rate 92.5%
Student mobility rate* 54%

*Proportion of students entering or leaving the school during the school year

Chicago Tribune Graphic; Source: Chicago Board of Education

Goudy Elementary School

Foster
Ashland Winthrop Sheridan
Montrose

Chicago

Making a point: *David LaRue works with 4th-grader Sokhom Nhem. LaRue tries to make a difference by sprinkling academics with lessons about life. He wants kids to realize that there are no jobs for people who cannot read.*

Where survival becomes the lesson of the day

*'My momma going to . . .
beat your butt.'*

T hird-grade teacher Mary Leahu is standing in the middle of Room 312, one shoe resting on a crumpled candy wrapper and her glasses slightly askew. Her face is pressed close to a page in the teachers' manual that suggests how to conduct the reading lesson for the day. The room smells like corn chips. The pencil sharpener is grinding.

At the supply cabinet, one student is handing out stacks of red construction paper to her friends.

On the chalkboard, another child has printed "kiss my ass."

"All right, we must read," Leahu announces, ready to begin the lesson. "David, read . . . David! . . . David?

Finally, she looks up from the page.

"Where is David?" Leahu asks no one in particular.

"He ain't here," explains Aretha Johnson, whose mouth is full of sunflower seeds. "He blowin' his bad breath on the door."

David is outside the classroom with his nose pressed against the door's glass window. He is laughing. Leahu moves toward him. He disappears. Then she pans the classroom and notices the chaos around her. She blinks as if caught in the glare of headlights. She freezes.

As part of an seven-month examination of the Chicago Public Schools, The Tribune spent nearly four months visiting the classrooms of Goudy Elementary in Uptown to see what public education has come to mean for the children whose futures are being silently but certainly shaped in one of city's 402 regular neighborhood grade schools.

Behind each classroom door at Goudy is a story about public education. And there are as many kinds of stories as there are kinds of teachers: inspiring, sad, effective, cruel, bewildered, even absurd.

Probably nothing has more to do with the kind of learning that takes place than the teacher's ability to manage a room of as many as 39 children.

In Room 312, Leahu heads to the pencil sharpener, where Victoria Brantley has been sharpening the same pencil for several minutes:

"You must do your reading," she tells Victoria.

"I got to sharpen my pencil."

"Your pencil is sharp," Leahu orders, pulling at Victoria's arm.

Victoria yanks her arm back, makes a face, then breaks off her pencil point.

"Guess it's broke now," Victoria says.

To the supply cabinet, where Serena Brown has been passing out construction paper until only a few sheets are left:

"Stop it," Leahu yells, grabbing Serena by the arm. "You cannot take paper from there."

"You don't touch me, my momma gonna sue you," Serena cries, slapping Leahu's hand with such force that the crack sounds all through the room. Leahu looks at the girl but does nothing. As she walks away, Aretha stands up and points:

"Yeah, and you touch me my momma going to come in here and beat your butt, yes she will."

While it is true that children from low-income families can pose a challenge to teachers, particularly when they live in an isolated world where lessons taught might not be reinforced in the home, in a truer sense many of these children are not that much different from children in any other school.

They respond to teachers they feel care and respect them. They challenge authority from time to time.

"I've had discipline problems before," admitted Leahu, who has

Latest gossip: Third graders in Mary Leahu's class catch up on gossip while a lesson is in progress. "What can I say? I'm here. I'm trying," Leahu says.

taught in the Chicago Public Schools for seven years. "But not this bad. What can I say? I'm here. I'm trying."

Three years ago, school board records show that Leahu received official warning at Bethune Elementary School on the West Side that her teaching performance was unsatisfactory, the first step toward a teacher's possible dismissal.

But the system gives teachers a second chance, and Leahu received an administrative transfer to another elementary school, where last year she received a "satisfactory" rating, the lowest acceptable.

Then she asked for a transfer to Goudy, at 5120 N. Winthrop Ave.

Her assignment was a room of 3d-graders, many of whom had already flunked. Leahu fought a daily battle that often dissolved into chaos and spilled into the hallways, interrupting other rooms. Her job was all the more difficult, Leahu said, because many of the children were being taught out of the same books they had the year before.

In March, more than halfway through the school year, Principal Thomas J. McDonald removed Leahu from her teaching assignment after an incident in which he said a girl assaulted a boy in the classroom and carved deep bleeding scratch marks in his face.

Leahu is now a "floating" teacher who assists in other classrooms in the afternoons.

But in the mornings, she still has the responsibility of teaching her group of academically deficient children how to read.

"We call this the 'bad room,'" one of her students, 3d-grader David Morris, explained one day. In full view of Mary Leahu, he tossed wet shards of red candy up at the ceiling in what appeared to be an experiment to see if they would stick.

"She thinks we're stupid. She gives us all the answers. She don't know how to make us act, so we tear up the place."

The sign on the door to Room 101 is printed in red, stenciled letters. It reads "Welcome to Our Little World."

Inside, the day's attendance is tallied on the chalkboard as "13 girls + 12 boys = 25 children. Not far from the equation, 1st-grade teacher Helen Harris is sitting cross-legged on the floor.

Gathered with her in a circle are 10 children eagerly watching as she thumbs through a stack of small manila cards on which she has written words that begin with "qu".

"That is absolutely perfect!" Harris says, smiling as she praises Larry Porter for recognizing how "quiet" is pronounced much differently than "quite."

The children are smiling, too.

There is a warm feeling about Helen Harris' classroom, a place where it is not unusual to find several different lessons simultaneously taking place. The children respond to both the structure and freedom in this room.

"Excuse me, Patricia," says Charles, who inadvertently bumped into his classmate while both were placing their papers on top of the work pile.

Patricia looked at him and smiled.

"First grade is my absolute favorite," explained Harris, a slender woman with a gravely voice who got her grammar school education at Goudy and now is in her 24th year of teaching at the school.

"Let me alone, I've got to alphabet

these," says a little girl who is trying to tell a classmate that she cannot be bothered because Harris has given her the job of putting the day's papers in order according to last names.

Responsibility is a lesson Harris teaches every day.

"I am not your mother, I am not your maid," she announces as she stands in the center of the classroom, pointing to the neglected Philadelphia Cream Cheese tubs that are used to hold paste. "Larry?" she asks. "Charles?" The two boys scamper to put their supplies away.

Her students always go home with marked papers. She wants them to learn from their mistakes.

"Be more careful," Harris wrote to Donna, who missed eight problems on her math paper, including 5−3=3.

"What happened?" she asked of Gennifer, who got 20 out of 30 wrong. "You did not think."

"Nice work!" was her message to Huong, who had only missed one problem.

"Almost Perfect!" Helen Harris wrote.

They call it "The Jail."

"Warden" Henry Caldwell stands up in front. Lean and mean. Hair clipped close.

"I'm the SOB of the third floor," he says.

His 33 sixth-graders are hunkered over their books. The talkative one is in segregation with her desk pushed way up against the front wall.

Room 309 is stripped down to the bare essentials. American flag in back. Nothing much on the walls. A few calendars with pictures of landscapes

dangle over chalkboards. Two lonesome globes rest on top of dusty bookshelves.

Caldwell is slight and stony-faced. In his hand is a ball point pen and a long slip of paper. On it, he makes checkmarks to tally episodes of unacceptable behavior. He'll need that paper at the end of the day.

Until he's ready, nobody leaves.

"Please, Mr. Caldwell," the assistant principal pleaded over the intercom one day. "Please bring your students down to lunch. We've got good chicken today."

He speaks in a dull monotone. Words drone. He gets impatient when the answers are wrong.

"Okay, if you're stupid sit there like a dummy," he tells a boy who cannot estimate a quotient.

Correct answers are often in chorus.

" ' . . . the wide white silence' and the 'black penciled on the snow.' Class, with a poem like this you have to . . .

(Chorus) "Think."

" . . . which means you have to use your . . ."

(Chorus) "Head."

" . . . and you need to use your head to use your . . ."

(Chorus) "Imagination."

Caldwell means business when he tallies those checkmarks at the end of the day. When he counts a lot of them, he puts the whole class "on punishment," which means he leads all 33 to the designated spot at the top of the north stairway, girls in one line and boys in the other.

Then they march. Down and up. Three flights down and three flights up.

Warden Caldwell marches right along with them, in front of kids who are gasping, sweating, who curse him

softly but who keep on marching.
Usually, for a half hour or more.

'Good morning, 301, and let's have them," 4th-grade teacher David LaRue says with an outstretched palm. He has positioned himself strategically beside the aquarium so they will see him when they bound into the room. The week before, 25 of his 37 students flunked their spelling test, which was unheard of because the class usually performs much better. So he ordered everyone to take the test home for a parent to sign.

"Sharena?"
"I forgot."
"Timothy?"
"Uhm, don't got it."
Three days had passed and only 16 tests had made it back.

LaRue deals with Tory Robertson, who is ready to hit the girl sitting in his seat. He takes attendance. He collects lunch money from those who pay. He leads the Pledge of Allegiance and sings the "Star-Spangled Banner" a little off key. He checks in calculators that went home overnight. He tries to find out more about the two missing math books. He tells Dawayne Holloway he

Walk this way: Sixth-grade teacher "Warden" Henry Caldwell marches with his students. The parade goes to the stairs at the end of the day if class deportment deteriorates. "I'm the SOB of the third floor," he says.

wants to speak to his mother because he's tired of him walking in late.

For the third time, he extends his deadline so the children can return a form with a parent's signature that will enable them to receive a free poster and a free book.

"It's time," Rodney Leggett announces as he jumps up from his seat. A chorus of chairlegs start scraping across the wooden floor.

The first 15 minutes of the school day have passed quickly.

More than half of his young students get up and leave.

All day long, LaRue's 37 students take part in a chaotic and often confusing game of public education musical chairs.

His classroom has become secondary to a maze of instructional programs,

Opportunity: While his students move in and out, David LaRue teaches whatever he can to whatever children are left over in his room.

some funded generously by the federal government, that are in place in the school because Goudy's students are poor readers, low achievers, ethnically diverse, and because they come from low-income homes.

While his students move in and out of his classroom and scatter through the building for a little of this and a little of that, LaRue teaches whatever he can to whatever children are left in his room.

He teaches a lot of lessons over and over again.

"There is no continuity to the school day," said LaRue, 28, a teacher who is frustrated by the ways of the public school system. "It's just various degrees of chaos, every day, all day long. Lessons just don't sink in.

"When I ask, I am told it is for the benefit of the children, but I don't see it," said LaRue, among whose accomplishments with his children is turning an F speller into the two-time champion of Room 301's spelling bee. "I don't see the gains."

LaRue tries to make a difference in the lives of his young students by sprinkling the academics with lessons about life. He wants them to realize that they don't have to live on welfare, but there are no jobs for people who cannot read.

One day, he sat down with a pencil and paper, did some figuring, and confirmed his worst suspicion—that the longest period in the entire school day that he has all of his 37 children together, uninterrupted and fresh enough to respond to his best shot, is 30 minutes.

Which means that David LaRue has his work cut out for him between 12:45 and 1:15.

The kids call Room 306 the "Psycho Ward."

Meet some of the boys assigned to this room:

There's Cinque King, the boy who punched the gym teacher.

And Antonio Robertson, a pencil-thin character who got in a fight with 3d-grade teacher Mary Leahu one day and knocked the glasses off her face.

Maurice Elliston is the feisty one who nearly gave a teacher a heart attack the day he smuggled an authentic-looking toy pistol into her room.

Arnaray Bibbs has been caught with a real weapon twice. Once Principal McDonald confiscated a kitchen knife the boy said he brought to school for "protection." The second time, McDonald called police after Arnaray threatened to kill a teacher who tried to make him do some work. The weapon was a pair of toenail clippers with a tiny knife on one end.

Sometimes they're bad on purpose. At least that's what their teacher has come to believe. "In a way, it's expected of them," explained Fani Cahill. " They

Attention: Fourth graders learn the value of following orders—the straightest line goes to the lunchroom first.

know they have an audience. A lot of it has to do with the chemistry of all of them being put together in one room."

The system deals with the most difficult children by evaluating them and using red ink to stamp their permanent record cards with the words "Child Study." The children are labeled "B-D" for behavior-disorder and placed in special classrooms.

This is much different from the way the system deals with teachers who have trouble in school. It tolerates them and even compensates for the weakness.

Though there are incidents, some of the boys do well when they fan out into the school's regular classrooms for reading classes. Principal McDonald believes that having all the boys in one room works against them. He would prefer to have them assigned to a regular class with the B-D teacher as a backup when they need help.

Hardly a day goes by when somebody isn't chasing these boys down the hallway. Sometimes it's McDonald, the security guards, or other students who tease the boys, calling them "psycho" or "brain-damage," a play on the label B-D.

Often, it was Cahill, a gifted teacher who in April took a personal leave.

Room 306 was often in an uproar. The kids swung brooms. Threw wastebaskets.

Two of them threatened to kill their bus attendant one day.

These boys cried when they lost a basketball game, threw snowballs at

pedestrians from their third-floor classroom window, but they sat quietly when Cahill told them a story about her life or when she read them a nursery rhyme.

Occasionally, they even let her teach.

Barbara Barajas tried bringing order in Spanish. In English. In Spanish again. She clapped her hands. She frowned. Then she walked over and flicked the lights on and off and ordered the children to sit, fold their hands, and put heads down.

"They just get crazy, and I have no idea of what else to do," Barajas explained as she stood helplessly in front of Room 204.

Barajas, who had taught in Texas, was new this year. She was not prepared for so many children with so much energy in one room. Hers was a class of 35 low-achieving 1st and 2d graders. She said school was in session three weeks before she received any books.

Not even two months into the school year, she quit.

On her last day, she received love notes and goodbye hugs from the children. After they left, she took a few minutes to pick candy wrappers off the floor and throw away a couple of broken pencils. Then she put on her coat, grabbed her purse and left.

On top of her desk sat the crate of teaching materials she brought with her from Texas.

"I don't want it," she said as she fled down the second-floor corridor.

"I don't know if I'll ever teach again."

It comes to this: Police take away two Goudy students after responding to a call about a disturbance. Principal Thomas J. McDonald once confiscated a kitchen knife from a student who said he brought it to school for "protection."

Ready to help: *Principal Thomas J. McDonald joins in a discussion with a parent (head on hand) of a student. He often visits students' homes.*

'Doc' will knock on any door to get the job done

'Come on, Caesar,
I'll take care of you.'

'**I**'m a lousy administrator, I'll admit to that," said Principal Thomas J. McDonald as he drove down Wilson Avenue in his mobile office, a dirty brown Peugeot that had two Hathaway ties and a copy of "Descartes' Dream" amid the rubble on the back seat.

"In my later years," explained the man who for two decades has been in charge of Goudy Elementary School, "I've tended to neglect the things I don't care that much about so I can spend more time on the things I like."

He slowed down a little and leaned forward to peer through the windshield. "I think this is it," he said, nodding toward a large apartment building on the south side of the street. He drove around the block to find a parking space. Then he bounded out of the car and took off down the sidewalk, white hair poking out from under a tweed cap and a slight stoop to his gait.

Throughout the Chicago Public Schools, there is no one more influential in shaping the day-to-day operation of a school than its principal.

On this afternoon, McDonald was six city blocks from his Uptown schoolhouse and a world away from the administrative tasks that he abhors. He was looking for one of his Goudy families, a mother who had moved with her five children after she could not scrape together the rent.

The building was the kind where the visitor has to be buzzed inside, and there was McDonald, this 65-year-old, well-dressed suburban gentleman with an ulcer, peering through a pair of half-glasses to scan mailboxes for the name Elliston. He couldn't find it so he tried his trick of pressing all of the buzzers. Even that didn't work. Finally, two men walked into the vestibule and when they were buzzed for entry, McDonald smiled slyly as he sneaked in.

"My boss ordered me not to do this," McDonald said as he started down the hallway. "He doesn't want me to go out into the community. But I ignore him. I learn something behind every door."

His face fell a little when he walked inside the apartment.

It was a tiny, one-bedroom space. Dark because the curtains had been drawn. A cockroach was crawling over food left out on top of the stove. Sommers Elliston, a 3d grader who had just walked the six blocks home from Goudy, was standing as he watched a small black-and-white television showing cartoons on a snowy screen. There was no chair for him to sit on. There was hardly room to walk. The small living area was crammed with three sets of bunk beds that accommodated five children and two adults.

McDonald had come looking for Janet Elliston, hoping to talk with her about her 12-year-old son, Maurice, one of the boys in the school's behavior-disorder classroom. He had become more unruly than usual that week. The principal had called the police after episodes in which the boy kicked his teacher, fought with a security guard and left McDonald redfaced after wrestling with him in his office.

Unlike the school system he works for, McDonald tries never to look at a child in isolation.

Janet Elliston had not yet returned home from her job as a day laborer, but a family friend in the apartment explained that the mother was keeping the children there on a temporary basis because she planned to move them all to California. It was a helpful insight, for it told McDonald a little something he did not know.

He visited for a while. Then he waved to the children and walked out past a cardboard box that served as a wastebasket and where 1st grader Essie Elliston's math paper, marked in red ink

with a perfect 100, was crumpled and covered with cracker crumbs.

When the door closed behind him, McDonald shook his head.

"You have to wonder how some of these children survive," he said as he zipped up his coat.

"You see, most of my teachers have never been in that apartment," McDonald said, a knowing look on his face.

"They have no idea how far some of these kids come to go to school."

McDonald is a legendary character in the Uptown neighborhood, the principal who runs his schoolhouse from the streets.

The system gives principals great leeway in how they operate. And the policy McDonald considers most effective in running his school was not developed by the Board of Education.

He calls it "knock on any door."

He pounds the pavement with the determination of a police detective. One day he's standing in the Red Rooster tavern on Argyle asking the man nursing a 10 a.m. beer if he's heard anything about a young truant who has run away from home. Another morning, he's sipping coffee with the street people at the counter of Don's grill trying to find out about the neighborhood squabble that the kids have resumed inside his school.

He is not the kind to sit in an office and talk about the staggering needs of his students while complaining that the system has cut his truant officer down to only once a week and cut his social worker to only twice a month.

He does not spend much time in his office at all.

His preoccupation is with doing whatever it takes to get children into the

In his element: "*Doc*" *loves all children. He doesn't care where they've come from, says a teacher.*

schoolhouse so they at least have a chance to learn.

"It's a question of priorities," McDonald explained one morning as he grabbed for his hat and coat. "The solution is often the problem in the public schools.

"You can't do anything for these children if you don't know where they come from, what they are like. No one else is going to do this," he said as he headed out the school's main entryway. "So I do a lot of it myself."

His daily sojourns take him to the sidewalks of Uptown, where he stops to talk to a young woman he suspected of working as a prostitute when she attended Goudy and who now has an eerie look about her with yellow, jaundiced eyes. She laughs when he reminds her of the time she stole a taxicab while a student at his school.

And it takes him up steps that have been encrusted with vomit and into hallways that reek with a curious mingling of urine, sweat, and leaking natural gas. Twenty years in the community have made him so familiar that he has no trouble convincing building engineers to let him into apartments with passkeys so he can see if the family he is looking for is still around.

He knows everybody by their nicknames—Sparkle, Juicy Lucy, Punkin, Turtle, and Hillbilly John.

They all call him "Doc."

It was McDonald who cultivated the nickname, actually, a moniker he uses not only for familiarity but also to poke fun at the doctorate of education that was necessary for his advancement through the ranks of the public school system but which he laughingly dismisses as "virtually useless" for

anything else.

His methods are a little unorthodox when he is out in the community.

He has been known to drag truant children out of closets and give them a forcible escort to school. He has taped notes to doors so the parent would know he was watching.

"In the warm weather," said Goudy teacher's aide Velma McLaurin, "you see ole Doc with a stick chasing after kids in the alley trying to get them in school."

On occasion, he has been known to kick a behind.

"I was mad as hell," McDonald explains, recalling an incident that he said took place on a warm spring day during one of his first years at Goudy.

"I took a kid out on the sidewalk, and I booted him as hard as I could. Then I looked around and saw all these people watching me from their porches and I thought, 'Oh, oh, what have I done now?' It was the '60s and here I was, this white man doing this to a black child.

"Then the funniest thing happened," McDonald remembers. "They all gave me a big round of applause."

Inside the schoolhouse, however, McDonald does not always enjoy such an enthusiastic following.

He's a little unorthodox there, too.

While it is often said that a public school is a reflection of its neighborhood, it is a reflection of its principal as much as anything else.

McDonald came to Goudy in 1967, and like any other principal in the system, he brought his own personality, his own eccentricities and his own style. He is an abstract thinker and a mathematician who often refers to himself as the "paradoxical principal."

Some of his teachers often have a difficult time coping with what that has come to mean.

"This school used to be a gorgeous melting pot," said teacher Ruby Smith. "We had an international festival where the parents would display things they made, and we would have a potluck and a program in the gym."

McDonald says he does not believe in such "showcase" activities.

"I've been here 19 years, and I still can't get used to it," said teacher Dan Griffin. "I like balanced discipline."

McDonald does not run a traditional disciplined school.

"You can't send a kid to the office for punishment," said 4th-grade teacher David LaRue. "They like to go to the office because they know they can play with Doc."

Eighth-grade teacher Bernice Eiland put it this way: "He loves all children. He doesn't care what or where they've come from. I don't think anybody questions that.

"But to work in this school, you got to be strong, you hear me? You got to be strong."

McDonald does not require that his teachers chart out lesson plans, which is customary in the public school system. He does not ask them to follow school board policy and assign homework, so not all of them do. When it comes right down to it, McDonald does not seem to believe in a lot of conventions that come with running a school.

"Let's see what's going on here!" he exclaimed one morning. All of a sudden, he grabbed hold of the edge of his desk and pushed so that his chair, on rollers, sailed back toward the public address system. Then he just started flipping buttons, his voice cutting into a series of rooms: "Are they behaving today, Mrs. Leahu?"

He spends a lot of time in the hallways, usually with a couple of children tugging at his hands. He is a benevolent yeller who one minute is screaming "Shut up! Mind your teacher!" to a gaggle of boisterous students and then the next minute is joking with them in the hall.

He wrestles with boys who are reluctant to talk to him by holding onto and yanking their thumbs and he randomly fishes through their pockets for "gyppers," paper clips that have been bent to the size of a quarter for free video games and the markers and shoe polish the kids use to scribble graffiti.

Occasionally, he confiscates real knives and toy guns.

"I violate their civil rights every day," McDonald explains.

Some of the older kids in the building laugh at his antics and try to take advantage of his kindness. They call him "crazy ole Doc."

Younger ones sometimes call him "Old McDonald" and they sing the song when they see him coming down the hall.

He doesn't mind any of it. Nor does he get upset when the children do not give him the kind of respect that is customary for a principal.

One afternoon, he was walking down the hallway and spotted 4th-grader Shawn McDowell with a piece of wood that doubles as a hall pass out of Room 301.

"Hey!" McDonald said in a voice that made it difficult to tell if his seriousness was in jest. "What are you doing with that stick?"

"I'm going to hit you in the ass," Shawn said playfully.

And he did.

Thomas J. McDonald, who is paid $55,975 a year, is one of the survivors in the Chicago Public Schools.

His 39 years of service have made him wise to the many failings of the system and he is skillful in the many manipulations that are often necessary when antiquated policies have little application in the day-to-day operation of a public school.

"All principals are liars," he says. "If anyone wanted to find out what I'm doing, they'd have to go through my desk." He laughs, looking down at the mishmash of papers, reports, and the ever-present stack of books on the philosophies of Rudy Rucker and Jean Piaget.

"In the public school system," McDonald explained, "you can fake almost anything."

The two Cambodian aides who are supposed to work with Cambodian children were observed doing a lot of other things, like mopping tables after lunch in a kindergarten classroom, watching a classroom while a teacher took a break and running the ditto machine.

"It's a violation," McDonald admitted when he was asked about such tasks after an auditor came through the school one day.

"But that's for me to let them do and for them to catch," he said. "They didn't find it."

And many administrative tasks that might ordinarily fall to the principal or the assistant principal are assumed by the two special reading teachers who are at Goudy because of the school's history of poor reading scores.

"You see," McDonald explained. "I have a system in place that allows me to spend time doing the things I like. . . . And I'm a good company man. My boss, Howard Sloan, wants us all to be good company men. Actually, there's only two things I really have to do when I run this school. One, I must never embarrass my boss and two, I must make him look good once in a while."

McDonald is usually quick to accommodate the most vocal complainers, particularly when he feels they are people who might be able to make life difficult for him.

But he is open about the fact that he sometimes finds ways to make life less than pleasant for a teacher with whom he is having a disagreement. He can have a hair-trigger temper, and when it goes off he sometimes yells at a teacher right in front of the class.

"I yell at her whenever I have the opportunity," McDonald said one day as he stopped in the third-floor hallway to look in on teacher Helen Manos in Room 310.

McDonald has virtually no say over what teachers are sent to Goudy. Manos was transferred from another school after having been suspended for three days on a charge of striking a child. She maintains it was an accident.

Manos is heavy and barely 5 feet tall. She walks with a cane. McDonald assigned her to a classroom that requires her to walk up and down three flights of stairs several times a day.

"I call that a challenge," McDonald said one day when asked about the classroom assignment. "If you give somebody enough of a challenge, maybe they'll quit."

Though he is diligent in cultivating connections with the families whose children go to Goudy, he is a master of illusion. He manages to keep them at arm's length when it comes to the operation of his school.

"What I've got here are unsophisticated parents," McDonald said. "They have no idea of the kind of power they could have. My friends in the suburbs tell me about parent groups and all their meetings, and I have to laugh.

"Actually," McDonald said. "I prefer it this way. It's easier for me to run the school."

McDonald's boss, District 2 Supt. Howard Sloan, voiced his support for the principal of Goudy School.

"I think he's quite a brilliant individual, and he certainly has a lot of opinions," said Sloan.

"I understand what he is trying to do. I applaud it. I think he does a nice job, an adequate job. He's pragmatic if you will, out in the hallways, that kind of thing."

After returning to Goudy one morning after presenting his annual principal's "Performance Objectives" to Sloan, McDonald took a copy of his report out of a folder.

"It's a fake," McDonald explained as he examined the 10-page document, in which he listed certain objectives and weighted each with the percentage of effort he would invest in each category.

McDonald, who tends to frustrate less abstract thinkers with his habit of equating all human behavior with mathematical principles, pointed to a category entitled "Improving School Pragmatics."

"He didn't even ask me what that meant," McDonald said, chuckling.

Then he flipped through the report and pointed out that all of his percentages added up to a total of 125 percent effort at Goudy School.

"He asked me why I said 125 percent," McDonald said, a sly grin coming over his face.

"And I said, 'Why, I always give you 100 percent, Mr. Sloan.' "

Though there have been some academic gains during his tenure, McDonald does not share the system's obsession with evaluating the children according to how they score on standardized tests.

"They tell us nothing that we don't know already," explained McDonald, "that children from low-income families tend to score lower. I'd like to throw out the testing program altogether and replace it with an Index of Decent Human Beings. I think that would tell us more about these kids in the long run."

McDonald hates to suspend students. So instead of suspending Antonio Robertson for hitting a classmate, McDonald *threatened* to suspend him.

"I ain't gonna be suspended," Antonio protested as McDonald held onto the boy's collar and tried to keep him from running after his classmate.

"I'm gonna come to school tomorrow. I'm gonna come to your stupid-assed school."

Sure enough, Antonio came to school.

Walking down the sidewalk one afternoon, McDonald waved at Debbie Gutshall, a Goudy graduate who said she dropped out in her freshman year of high school. She was cradling a sack of groceries.

"Say," McDonald said, stopping to talk with her about her daughter, the second generation of that family to pass through his school. "Candy is doing real well."

"That's right, Doc," Gutshall said, smiling. "I make sure she's there every day."

McDonald smiled to himself as he walked down the sidewalk.

"I was always after her, trying to get her to come to school. Now, you see, she wants something better for her daughter."

"Mom talks about Doc," said Candy Gutshall, an 8th grader. "She tells me about when she went to school. She does not want me to make the same mistakes."

McDonald is one to give bus fare or lunch money to kids who say they need it. If a child is hungry, McDonald will often feed him, especially if he passes along little tidbits, like who is drawing graffiti in the bathroom and in what locker the shoe polish and the markers are being stashed.

It is difficult for McDonald to turn any child away.

Lunch did not agree with a 1st-grade boy one day, and he got sick all over his blue jeans. The school office was in a panic. No one was answering the boy's home phone. He was crying. The smell was terrible.

Then McDonald came walking down the hall.

The black-haired boy looked down at his pants. Then he looked up at McDonald, a pathetic look on his face. "Come on, Caesar," McDonald said, "I'll take care of you."

McDonald knew the boy's family. He knew where the child's baby-sitter lived.

So he put on his hat and his coat and he walked the boy safely to his sitter's home.

Thomas J. McDonald said he plans to retire at the end of this school year.

Window of despair: *A Du Sable High student looks elsewhere. Pupils are trapped in a system run by political appointees.*

No clout, no concern: The bottom line is no education

'Most children are merely being warehoused'

The Chicago Public School system is a case of institutionalized child neglect.

Instead of working to nurture productive citizens, the guardians of the system divert themselves with a game of politics, risking the futures of hundreds of thousands of children.

They get away with it because these are the children of the poor and powerless, parents isolated from the economic and political clout they need to make the system work for them.

School administrators and board members, aldermen, mayors, legislators and teachers have programmed the system so that it responds to their needs but betrays generations of children in the process.

Not all of the 595 Chicago public schools are failures, not all of the 28,675 teachers or 419,537 students. There are flashes of excellence, teachers who care and children who learn.

But success is the exception. The truth is that most of the children, mired in poverty and trapped in the politics of neglect, aren't taught to read or do arithmetic well enough to make it in the workplace.

Hardly anyone expects them to do anything but fail.

At Robeson High School, 6835 S. Normal Ave., freshmen were gathered for an assembly and asked about the future.

"We'll do what everyone expects us to do," one boy shouted out. "We'll go on welfare and abuse our children."

This is the way the lives and expectations of too many of Chicago's children are being shaped. And the consequences are grave.

The schools have the potential to break the cycle of urban poverty and despair. But nearly half the students drop out before finishing high school. A fourth of those who do graduate enter the job market at a 6th-grade reading level. The cycle goes unbroken.

A seven-month examination of the Chicago Public Schools by The Tribune found a desperate tangle of problems.

It begins with the extraordinary needs of the children, but it does not end there. Two-thirds of them live in poverty, and many come to school with a background of deprivation that would make learning difficult under the best of circumstances.

They encounter teachers from an ingrown, aging and protected work force of uneven ability, qualification and motivation.

Pupils and teachers alike are trapped in a system inadequately administered by political appointees and career bureaucrats whose concern for comfort, survival and status quo strangle the system.

If innovative administrative ideas ever did surface, they would meet the opposition of a union that has dominated the educational agenda for two decades.

There is not enough money to go around, and the children always seem to have the last claim.

The only people who could help don't. Neither Chicago's City Council, nor the city's delegation to the General Assembly, nor other local and state officeholders care enough about these children's future to take a political risk.

"Right now, most children are merely being warehoused in school buildings," Greta Carl, the mother of a high school student, testified at a legislative hearing. "I am frightened when I think about the future."

As the Chicago Board of Education has scrounged over the years for money to pay employees and end recurring strikes, the city's neighborhood school system has withered.

The best of the students are drawn to elite magnet schools, where teachers are selectively chosen, classes are challenging and books and equipment are ample and up to date.

The rest of the children—three-fourths of them—are relegated to neighborhood schools.

In middle-class neighborhoods, some of these schools still function well,

thanks to the efforts of parents.

But in many of the impoverished, crime-torn neighborhoods whose children have the greatest needs, education takes place in a chaotic, dehumanizing environment—crumbling buildings scarred by graffiti, battered equipment and scattered trash.

At some schools, officials refuse to put toilet paper in the student lavatories, saying the children misuse it.

A school day might consist only of hour after hour of mind-numbing rote, drilled from tattered and out-of-date texts—when there are enough to go around.

At some schools, children are penned inside all day, denied recess and deprived of the mind-stretching stimulus of music, art or extracurricular activities.

"It's a facade," says Fred Shudnow, who is struggling to teach a split 5th-6th grade class at Bethune Elementary School, 3030 W. Arthington St.

"They say to these kids, 'You've got the teachers and a school like anybody else.' But these kids are behind. They need extra help. I've got the slowest kids, and I've got 35 of them. It should be more like 20, but the board doesn't see that. These kids need tutors, more help.

"They should do something to get them off welfare, not guarantee that they'll stay on it."

In a combined 7th-8th grade classroom at Bethune, a 14-year-old girl is pregnant for the third time. A 15-year-old boy was the neighborhood's busiest drug pusher, his teacher says, until his best friend was shot and killed over drugs last year—right across the street

The Chicago Public Schools

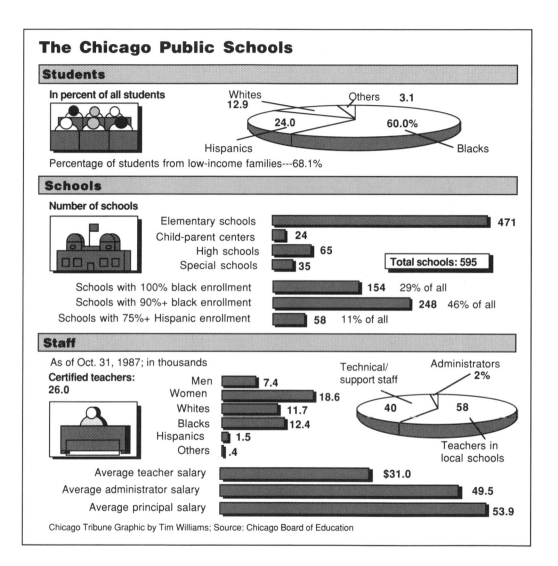

Students

In percent of all students

Whites 12.9 — Others 3.1

Hispanics 24.0 — Blacks 60.0%

Percentage of students from low-income families---68.1%

Schools

Number of schools

Elementary schools — 471
Child-parent centers — 24
High schools — 65
Special schools — 35

Total schools: 595

Schools with 100% black enrollment — 154   29% of all
Schools with 90%+ black enrollment — 248   46% of all
Schools with 75%+ Hispanic enrollment — 58   11% of all

Staff

As of Oct. 31, 1987; in thousands

Certified teachers:
26.0

Men — 7.4
Women — 18.6
Whites — 11.7
Blacks — 12.4
Hispanics — 1.5
Others — .4

Technical/support staff — 40
Administrators 2%
Teachers in local schools — 58

Average teacher salary — $31.0
Average administrator salary — 49.5
Average principal salary — 53.9

Chicago Tribune Graphic by Tim Williams; Source: Chicago Board of Education from the school.

Another student sleeps with five other children on three piled-up mattresses in an unheated apartment. During the winter, the boy often came to school smelling of urine because it was too cold for the smaller kids to get up and go to the bathroom at night.

Asks teacher Corla Hawkins, "How can you learn when people tell you that you smell of piss, and you do?"

The results of the neglect and despair are readily evident in the numbers that measure student achievement in Chicago:

• Forty percent of Chicago high school students flunk at least two major courses each year. That's the average, for 111,891 teenagers. At Crane High School, the failure rate reaches 65 percent; for freshmen at Marshall High, it hits 76 percent.

• Half of the city's 65 high schools place in the bottom 1 percent of U.S. schools in the ranking of how their students scored last year on the American College Test (ACT).

• Barely half of Chicago's high school students graduate. The rest drop out. At some schools, such as Austin and Roosevelt, fewer than 15 percent of the students graduate with their class.

• The average Chicago high school graduate looking for a job reads about as well as the average American 8th grader. One of every four such graduates reads only as well as the average 6th grader.

These children do learn some things in Chicago Public Schools. They learn that many adults can go through the motions of their teaching jobs with little

or no skill and still be well paid—an average of $31,000 a year, with summers off.

They learn that many people don't care about them—about whether they go to school, or whether they learn anything while there. They learn that their education is less important than the battles between the school board and the teachers' union that have resulted in nine strikes in 18 years.

They learn that, for society at large, their parents don't count for very much—and neither do they.

School Supt. Manford Byrd Jr. says the ultimate responsibility for failure rests with the children.

"The overarching goal of my administration," Byrd wrote in the program budget for the 1986-87 school year, "is continual and measured program improvement to make certain that every child has a chance for a quality education."

Asked about his use of the word "chance," Byrd said: "The challenge is to make a connection, to get where the kid is. But, when you're all done, the learner must learn for himself or herself. In the end, the learner must undergo the immersion, the exercises.

"I don't think we can excuse the learner. There's a certain amount of motivation necessary, a certain amount of want-to."

But it's difficult for children to motivate themselves when many teachers, administrators and parents have given up. An attitude of hopelessness pervades the school system, often expressed with a shrug.

"We're a general high school," says Elaine Thigpen, head of counseling at

Calumet High School, 8131 S. May St. "We have 2d- and 3d-grade readers. We must educate the mass.

"We hope to do better, but we won't die if we don't."

The Chicago schools have been a political playground since the first public school opened in the city in 1834.

As Chicago developed into a city of factories, stockyards and segregated ethnic neighborhoods, the public schools served the children of immigrants and the patronage needs of the political machine. The city's rich sent their children to elite private academies, and the political leadership, all white and largely Roman Catholic, sent theirs to parochial schools.

Although Chicago's political structure has shifted to black control, one thing hasn't changed: The power structure still has little personal involvement in the public schools.

School Board President Frank Gardner, although a public school teacher and administrator for 35 years, and his wife, Elaine, also a public school teacher, sent their three children to parochial schools.

Mayor Eugene Sawyer's three children went to a private elementary school, and two also went to private high schools.

The children of Mayors Richard J. Daley and Jane M. Byrne went to parochial schools. State Rep. John P. Daley (D., Chicago) and Cook County State's Atty. Richard M. Daley have continued the tradition.

Only 15 of the city's 50 aldermen sent their children solely to public schools, a Tribune survey found. Thirteen aldermen—of whom 12 are white—sent their children exclusively to private schools. The remainder enrolled their children in a mix of public and private schools, or have no children who have reached school age.

"We're Catholic, and we want the religious instruction," said Ald. Edward Burke (14th), explaining why his four children attend parochial schools.

Burke paused, then added: "Nobody in his right mind would send kids to public school."

The most blatant use of Chicago public schools as an instrument of racial politics and social isolation came in the late 1950s, when the school board erected mobile classrooms and scheduled double shifts at crowded black schools rather than transfer black children to primarily white schools.

White children were a majority in the public schools then. But amid the racial tensions of the 1960s and 1970s, the parents of tens of thousands of children, fearful of busing proposals, transferred them to private schools or packed up and moved to the suburbs.

It has often been called white flight.

But a more apt term might be bright flight. A similar exodus of middle-class black children has taken place, leaving the public schools with the toughest children to teach.

The exodus, along with a drop in the birth rate, resulted in a public school enrollment decline of nearly 28 percent over 18 years—to 419,537 in 1987 from 580,292 in 1969.

Today, blacks make up 60 percent of the enrollment, Hispanics 24 percent and whites 12.9 percent; the other 3.1 percent are mostly Asians and American Indians.

This is out of whack with the overall city population—about 42 percent black, 41 percent white and 17 percent Hispanic.

It is even more out of whack with the people who hold the ultimate political power, those registered to vote: 49 percent white, 42 percent black and 7 percent Hispanic.

The disparity is so pronounced that some state legislators from city districts have hardly any constituents with an immediate interest in the schools.

In Democratic State Rep. Douglas Huff's impoverished West Side district, 25,375 children go to public schools. In the largely white, Southwest Side district of House Speaker Michael Madigan (D., Chicago), only 3,327 children do.

In that respect, Madigan is representative of his community. He didn't attend public schools, and his two school-aged children go to parochial schools.

Madigan, who controls the Democratic House majority, has a stock response to questions about any increase in school taxes: "I'm not convinced it's necessary."

Says Patricia O'Hern, a white Board of Education member from the Southwest Side: "As whites left the city, people started to assume the school system was all black or minority, so therefore they lost interest and stopped caring.

"That's when they should have been most interested, because these are the kids who need it the most. This is important to every person who lives in this city. This is their school system. This is their future."

The lack of interest by politicians, the lack of commitment of administrators and teachers, the lack of unity among parents have combined to isolate the school system to such an extent that, by default, it has become the battleground for the two groups that are clear about their goals.

On one side is a comfortably entrenched school bureaucracy, set on maintaining its status and the status quo.

On the other is an acrimonious Chicago Teachers Union, intent on wringing as much money out of the school board as possible and protecting its members.

The politicians' main goal has been to avoid a rupture in the great school machinery that employs 42,000 people, more than work for the City of Chicago. Those ruptures have never had anything to do with educating students.

"Politically and economically, the only pressure people have is just to keep that machinery going, even if it's not doing the best job, because too many jobs are at stake if it doesn't continue in operation," said George Munoz, a former school board president.

Mayor Richard J. Daley played the game to avoid teachers' strikes, not always successfully, by flat-out ordering the school board to grant pay raises with money it didn't have. Then, Daley would go to the legislature for the money. Sometimes he got it, sometimes he didn't.

When he didn't, he started a time bomb that exploded in 1979, three years after he died. The schools went broke.

Payless paydays for teachers sprung politicians into action. Gov. James Thompson held city and state leaders hostage for three days to get a rescue plan. It included a new School Finance Authority, given the power to stop the Board of Education from spending money it didn't have.

"That authority was created because the employees did not receive a paycheck on a timely basis," Munoz said. "Do we see that reaction when we hear that 40 percent of the students are dropping out?"

School board headquarters has traditionally been an extension of the mayor's office.

The mayor appoints the 11 board members. The mayor tells them if they can ask the state legislature for a tax increase. Sometimes mayors have allowed the board to go hat in hand to Springfield, then quietly sent a signal to legislators to kill the bid for money.

The school board can seek a tax increase by a referendum of city voters, but it has avoided that route for 20 years out of fear that the campaign would turn into a debate on the effectiveness of the schools.

The tax rate for the Board of Education has increased by only 2 percent since 1977, according to a League of Women Voters study. In the same period, the Chicago Park District's rate rose by 19 percent, Cook County government's by 42 percent and the Chicago City Colleges' by 106 percent.

The Chicago schools couldn't get a significant tax increase for 15 years until 1983, when Harold Washington became the first mayor in years to openly support higher local school taxes. The legislature approved a 50-cent increase in the education fund tax rate, restoring a cut made three years earlier when the

School Finance Authority was created.

When the legislature narrowly approved that tax measure, it exposed the racial schism that is an underlying cause of the isolation of Chicago's schools.

Every black lawmaker from Chicago supported the tax increase. But nearly every white lawmaker from Chicago voted against it, and to get the measure passed Washington and his allies had to cajole the support of Downstate legislators.

In Springfield, Chicago's schools are just one token in the never-ending game of political tradeoffs.

Gov. Thompson likes to say that education is his No. 1 priority and that he shares the anguish of other Chicago parents when strikes close the schools. His 9-year-old daughter, Samantha, attends a magnet school on the North Side.

But the state has slowly starved Chicago and other Illinois schools by reducing its overall support for education.

Senate Minority Leader James "Pate" Philip (R., Wood Dale) is one of the main players. Philip is the Du Page County Republican Party chairman, and when he refers to the Chicago public schools, he talks of "down there."

"The caliber of teachers leaves a lot to be desired," he says. "Some of the better teachers are afraid to go down there."

Many suburban and Downstate legislators use the term when talking about the city's schools. They also use terms like "sinkhole" and, occasionally, "black hole."

Thompson, after vetoing a school funding bill last fall, said: "I'm a parent and I care about public education in Chicago, but we can't keep throwing money into a black hole."

Whenever used, people rush to explain that it refers to the cosmic phenomenon that swallows up stars and is not a slur against the race of many of Chicago's students. But race never is far from the surface in any school discussion.

Philip was surprised to learn that city students' reading scores, though still far below national averages, are higher than in the mid-1970s.

"That's hard to believe," he said, "because you had more white kids in school then."

Other Springfield nicknames for Chicago schools include "cash cow" and "money machine." But budget data call them otherwise.

In the 1985-86 school year, the city's school system had total revenues from state, local and federal sources of $3,957 per enrolled student, nearly $800 less per pupil than the average suburban district.

This is true even though Chicago gets extra state funds designed, by law, to make educational opportunity roughly equal for all children in the state. But these funds do not come close to meeting the challenge of educating the children of poverty who flock to the city's schools.

Philip has proposed legislation, dubbed by opponents as a reverse-Robin Hood bill, that would take money from school districts with low achievement-test scores, such as Chicago, and give it to districts with high marks.

A school district report card

	New York	Los Angeles	Chicago	Miami	Houston	U.S. average
Student attendance	85.2%	89%	91%	92.7%	95%	94.3%
Per pupil expenditure	$5,585	$2,646	$3,225	$3,188	$2,908	$3,752
Average SAT score	807	824	892	860	862	906
Teacher-pupil ratio						1-17.8 (combined)
Elementary	1-18.3	1-33	1-30	1-18	1-24	
Secondary	1-15.2	1-36	1-28	1-18	1-28	
Average teacher salary	$37,756	$35,000	$31,058	$30,336	$24,790	$26,551
Enrollment	938,606	589,099	419,537	243,690	194,389	--
Drop-out rate	30.7%	34%	48%	30%	40%	25%

Chicago Tribune Graphic; Sources: "Public Schools: USA" by Charles Harrison, Education Business magazine, individual school districts, U.S. Department of Education, Education Research Service

"It's both a race and a class issue," says G. Alfred Hess, executive director of the Chicago Panel on Public School Policy and Finance, a citizens group.

"We would have a state formula for funding schools that was more beneficial to Chicago if race and class weren't so important in this state."

For an illustration of how provincialism and partisan politics combine to work against the schools, consider the case of State Rep. Andrew McGann.

McGann was miffed last year when the school board decided to reopen John Crerar School in his Southwest Side neighborhood. The board wanted to ease crowding at nearby schools, but McGann contended that the reopening would be an inconvenience for the Chicago Park District, which was using the building.

In the old days, McGann, a Democrat, would have won because he was an ally of Mayor Daley. But the old days are gone. The board voted to reopen Crerar.

McGann didn't give up.

Early this month, McGann joined Republicans to defeat two bills that would have allowed the school board to continue an existing tax for school rehabilitation.

McGann says he voted against the bills because the school board hadn't fully explained how it would use the money.

State Rep. Alfred Ronan (D., Chicago), a sponsor of one of the bills, said he couldn't discern McGann's motive. But he knew what the Republicans were up to.

"The Republicans told me they want-

ed another bargaining chip with the City of Chicago," Ronan said.

In other words, Republican lawmakers were willing to jeopardize the schools' building plan in the hope of winning a concession from Mayor Sawyer on other matters. That's how the game is played.

Because of the public outrage over the length of the last school strike, Chicago schools are getting some deep scrutiny.

Some of the more influential players in the politics of education have begun to talk publicly about taking steps to make the system work like it's supposed to.

For example, corporate leaders have become increasingly outspoken on the need to improve the quality of high school graduates, and some are edging toward support for increasing taxes for schools.

The president of the Chicago Teachers Union, Jacqueline Vaughn, has conceded that the board won't be able to meet its contract obligations to teachers this fall without financial help from the legislature. The union has insisted in the past that the board could find money to raise teachers' pay whether or not any new cash was coming from Springfield.

But any movement will have to overcome decades of political inertia.

Republican lawmakers have already quietly served notice that they won't agree to the financial demands accompanying various proposals to improve the schools without a Democratic agreement to shift a little more money away from Chicago.

If that happens, playground politics

will claim another victory.

At Goudy Elementary School, 5120 N. Winthrop Ave., Mrs. Kaye is gentle yet firm with the 22 children in her morning kindergarten. Her classroom is warm and pleasant. The children like to be there.

"I know that this room is probably nicer than many of their apartments," she says, "so I try to make it as comfortable for them as I can."

Mrs. Kaye is Georgia Kotsiopoulos. She has been teaching at Goudy for nearly a quarter of a century. She evaluates the children with a practiced eye.

Four are Cambodian and speak little English. Six others already are falling behind in their work. One child has a history of being abused. Three have speech impediments. Many come from families so poor that they lacked warm clothing to fend off the bitter cold of midwinter.

These 22 children are part of Chicago's future, members of the high school class of 2000. They will be entering the work force as the new century dawns.

Mrs. Kaye is asked how they will do as they go through the Chicago Public Schools over the next 12 years.

"The average," she says, "will survive."

Status quo: *The political structure has shifted to black control, but one thing hasn't changed: Children of power brokers don't attend public school. School Board President Frank Gardner's children went to parochial schools.*

100 students per teacher made learning a challenge

Chicago Public Schools have had troubles since the beginning.

In 1897, Hannah Belle Clark, a doctoral student in sociology at the University of Chicago, noted in her dissertation, "The Public Schools of Chicago: A Sociological Study," that the school system was ignoring the children of families living in poverty and the children of foreign-born immigrants.

"You may search the records in vain to find any explicit reference to these conditions or to any need for special adaptation of the curriculum to foreign clientage," Clark wrote.

"They gain little or no insight into the workings of the society in which they live, the dependence of every man on every other man, the relations of groups of men to each other. They do not learn how Chicago is fed or clothed, and not clearly how it is governed."

Classrooms were overcrowded even then, and as now, there wasn't enough money to do much about it. Lack of money has always been an issue in the public schools. So has race.

The first public school in Chicago was opened in 1834 in a Presbyterian church. Two years later, school officials spent $200 to build the first schoolhouse—but they had to borrow the money.

By 1843, the city had eight public school teachers and 818 public school students—a ratio of more than 100 students per teacher. Sixteen years later, some classrooms had as many as 150 students "with four or five little children on a seat built for two," according to Supt. William Wells.

The years immediately before and during the Civil War brought an influx of blacks to Chicago, and in 1863 the City Council passed the Black School Law that segregated black and white children. The law was repealed two years later.

By the turn of the century, the enforcement of child-labor and compulsory education laws had boosted enrollment, further crowding classrooms. In 1905, 11,000 children were on double-shift classes, and the school board voted to erect wooden "portable" schoolrooms next to schools.

Politics is another constant factor in Chicago schools. By the late 1920s, the system was riddled with political appointees. Janitors, school clerks and truant officers were among 2,500 employees whose jobs were doled out by ward bosses.

While the patronage rolls grew, the school system slipped into a financial morass. By 1927, it was broke. Then came the Depression.

Things didn't get back on track until after World War II, but by then, another black exodus from the South was under way, crowding the city's classrooms.

Supt. Benjamin C. Willis embarked on a huge construction program that was geared to do more than simply provide additional classrooms. It was designed to keep black students segregated in South and Near West Side neighborhoods, rather than transfer them to uncrowded schools in white areas of the city—such as Mayor Richard J. Daley's Bridgeport—where blacks were not welcome.

But the building program couldn't keep up with the booming enrollment, so Willis scheduled double shifts at some black schools and added mobile classrooms, which came to be known as "Willis Wagons."

In 1962, the National Association for the Advancement of Colored People filed an anti-segregation suit. To avoid a court battle, school officials named a commission to develop a desegregation plan that was subsequently approved in principle by the board, but never implemented.

Nonetheless, fears of court-ordered busing, fueled by real estate panic-peddlers, were convincing many whites to transfer their children to private schools or to move their families to the suburbs.

And, as the number of whites in the system went down, so did the amount of local money available for the schools.

In 1964, Robert J. Havighurst was hired to conduct a study.

In a report that rings true almost a quarter of a century later, he discussed the difficulty of teaching youngsters from low-income families, while stressing the vital importance of doing so.

"The future of democracy depends on our ability to do this," Havighurst warned. "Even in the narrowest economic sense, we need the human resources that these children represent.

"Furthermore, if we cannot find ways to educate them for economic and social competence, we will pay several times over in the future in costs of unemployment, dependency, delinquency and crime. Lack of money is accepted too easily, even by those closest to the situation, as a reason for not doing even those things which are already known to bring substantial results . . .

"The responsibility for this situation, of course, does not belong to the Board of Education alone, but to citizens and leadership at every level from which greater resources could come . . .

"Until all of these are willing to give more than lip service to the idea that education is an investment and that it is better to spend now than pay later for social misfits, we will continue to pay the cost of our failure to educate the majority of our culturally deprived children."

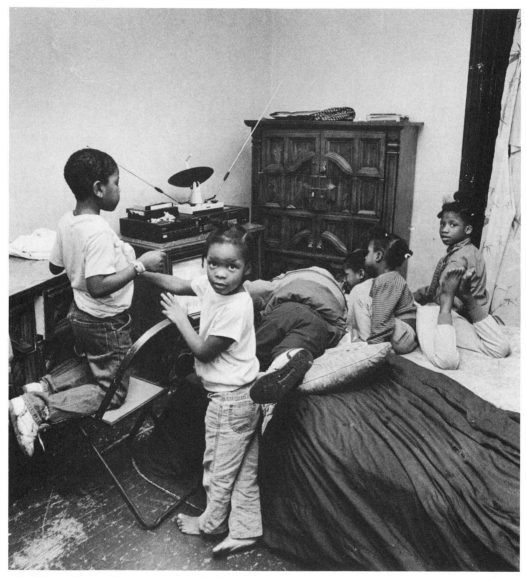

15 children, 1 home: *Six youngsters watch TV in a bedroom of the apartment where Antonio Robertson lives with 14 other children.*

For many poor kids, home is a place with no books

*'Sometimes, it's like
I'm teaching French'*

The stairwell was dark and the steps groaned as teacher Fani Cahill ventured into the rundown apartment building in Uptown, the place that one of her students knows as home. On the second floor, she knocked firmly on a door.

It opened just wide enough for 12-year-old Antonio Robertson to poke his head out.

"Oh, man," the boy said, scowling.

"I told you I was coming," said Cahill. "I told you I would be here to talk to your mother about what's been going on with you at school."

Antonio's mother, Alberta Robertson, appeared at the door. She looked at Cahill. Then she eyed her son.

"It's good to see you, Miss Cahill," she said, smiling tentatively. "Come on in."

Visiting the homes and classrooms of the children who attend one of Chicago's 402 regular elementary schools reveals that the children's family and school environments are desperately at odds. And the children are caught in the middle.

As part of a seven-month examination of the Chicago Public Schools, The Tribune spent nearly four months with the children of Goudy Elementary, 5120 N. Winthrop Ave.

Antonio lives only a block from Goudy, but like most of the children who depend on the public school system, he has to cross great distances to get to school.

His home is a dark, three-bedroom apartment that is shared by two families. He is one of 15 children who live there.

He does not have his own bed.

Antonio is short and wiry, a lively boy known as "Pooh" who has a quick wit and the kind of street smarts that come with living a lot in just 12 years. Part of him is tough, a lot of mouth. Part of him begs to be a child.

Cahill was visiting because it had been a particularly bad week at school for Antonio, who has repeatedly gotten into the kind of trouble that attracts the police.

One morning of this week, he had bolted out of Goudy with two buddies and skipped the better part of the day. Another time, he had fought with his classmates, then slipped down the hall to Room 312. There, he got into an argument with 3d-grade teacher Mary Leahu and knocked the glasses off her face.

"Sometimes, I don't know what to do with the boy," Alberta Robertson said as she walked over to turn down a blaring stereo. She explained that Antonio had become increasingly difficult since his 15-year-old brother was murdered last

August when the family was living in the Henry Horner Homes on the West Side.

"Pooh was getting out of hand in the projects," Robertson said. "I wanted to get out and get something better."

So they moved to this crowded apartment in Uptown, doubling up with another family to meet the rent.

Robertson sat down on one end of the couch. Cahill sat on the other. With his head down, Antonio sat in between.

The only light in the living room came from a small lamp. Posters from the Chicago Bears and the Chicago Transit Authority decorated the room. A raincoat dangled from a nail in the wall.

"It was not a mistake," Cahill told Antonio's mother. "He went down and hit the teacher in the face."

"What the hell is the matter with you?" Robertson asked, turning to look at her son. "What you want to go and do that for?"

"Speak up, Antonio," Cahill said.

Antonio said nothing. His nostrils flared.

"Mrs. Robertson, I am very concerned," said Cahill, who, like the Robertson family, is black. "Antonio somehow thinks he is not going to live long. He cannot think about the future. He's very upset about his brother's death.

"He says, 'When I get killed, boy, I'm gonna have the biggest funeral,' and I tell him he's just going to be another nigger dead. We've got a serious problem here, Mrs. Robertson. I want Antonio to make it. What should we do?"

The mother shook her head and was silent.

"I can't do nothin' with him," she fi-

nally said, her voice soft. "You might as well just put him away."

Cahill sighed. Then she looked hard at her student.

"Antonio," Cahill said, tugging at his arm. "Do you want to be put away?"

The boy said nothing.

"Look at your mother," she said. "Tell her you don't want to be put away."

He looked down.

"Antonio!," Cahill yelled. "They *can* put you away, do you know that? You won't get out till you're 18. And you ain't as big as a knittin' needle. You'll come out walkin' like a sissy. Do you know that?"

Antonio frowned.

With her arms crossed, Robertson stared at her son as she and Cahill talked for a few more minutes.

Then Cahill gathered up her things and headed for the door. Antonio held it open, but she paused before walking through.

"Until you learn to love yourself, I'm going to love you," Cahill whispered as she put an arm around his shoulders. "We are going to work together, you and I."

Antonio smiled weakly. His lips were trembling.

But he did not cry.

One of the underpinnings of the American system is the belief that its public schools provide a stepping stone to a better life.

But as effective as some of Chicago's elite public magnet schools are for the children of motivated families, the public school system fails utterly in meeting the challenge of educating the students left behind, a staggering number of whom might be at risk of failure from the very first day they walk through the schoolhouse doors.

These very children are part of the system's problem. Many come from desperately poor and unstable families, lacking positive role models, raised by parents who work rarely, if at all, and who move several times a year in the search of affordable housing.

Some children come to kindergarten still not toilet trained. There are 1st graders who come from homes where there is so little nurturing that they haven't learned colors and numbers. Eight-year-olds who tear pages out of books for toilet paper because they come from homes where there never have been books. Sixth-graders who don't know offhand how many inches there are in a foot because they have never worked with a ruler. Pre-teens who are mystified by the most common nursery rhymes and guess that "Humpty Dumpty" is a rap.

Few of these children have ever been to the zoo.

Few of these children have parents who have much schooling themselves. And these adults are barely prepared to help their children learn, much less to make demands of college-educated teachers and school administrators in an effort to get better schooling for their children.

Yet these impoverished children, who need so much and can be so difficult to teach, are the ones who have no option but to depend on public schools that have the least to offer.

With every scramble to scrape together the money to give teachers a raise to settle a strike, these schools lose a little more.

It is early in elementary school when a child is either turned on to the idea of an education or is forever lost. And at a school like Goudy, so much has been taken away that there is not a lot to keep the children interested unless teachers go way beyond what the system requires of them.

Classes in art and music are long gone. There are no extra-curricular activities. This year, the links to the parents were cut back—the school now gets a truant officer once a week and a social worker only twice a month.

School is a place where as many as 39 Goudy students are crammed into a classroom for the 5½-hour school day. They get no recess, but they do get tattered and out-of-date textbooks that are often in short supply.

Goudy's children come from families so uniformly poor that 98 percent of them qualify for the federal government's free lunch program.

A generation or two ago, many of these children might have left school at an early age to work in an economy that needed unskilled people willing to dig holes by hand or carry heavy things around. But now machines do that, and there is almost no demand for the unskilled, so these children must depend on the schools for whatever hope they have for a better life.

Three decades ago the majority of the student population was white and came from middle-class or working-class homes. Since then, after the racial turmoil of the 1960s and 1970s drove many children out of the public schools, the student population has changed dramatically.

Today, a full 68 percent of the 419,537 children enrolled in the public school system are poor. Overwhelmingly, they are minority: Sixty per cent are black, 24 percent are Hispanic, 2.9 per cent are Asian, and .2 per cent are American Indian or Alaskan; 12.9 per cent are white.

However dramatic this change in the nature of the challenge, the system has changed little in response.

"The schools have always been a middle-class institution with middle-class values," said Michael Bakalis, dean of the School of Education at Loyola University, observing that there is a fundamental conflict between the expectations of the institution and the grim realities of the children of poverty.

While it is unrealistic to think that school can be all things to all children, the job of the institution is to teach. Teachers and school administrators often throw up their hands and ask how the schools are supposed to make a difference when so much is lacking in the home.

School Supt. Manford Byrd Jr., for one, places final responsibility for learning on the children, rather than on the school system.

"The learner must learn for himself or herself," he says.

Not everyone shares his view.

"The school is called upon to play a parent role to compensate for a lack of support," said John McDermott, program chairman of the City Club of Chicago and former editor and publisher of the Chicago Reporter, an investigative newsletter that focuses on racial issues.

"We are losing a whole generation because of the inability of the school system to respond to the children," he said.

This is true of every urban school district in the country with a significant poor population. No American school system has found a way to teach impoverished children effectively and consistently. But a Tribune survey of other major cities found that Chicago lags badly in an emerging national effort to find approaches that work.

"You look at these kids and it's so frustrating," said Henry Caldwell, who teaches 6th grade at Goudy.

"You think, 'I'm teaching and they're not learning,' and you really struggle with that.

"Eventually, you realize that teaching is just not enough."

'Give me the parents of these children," says teacher Fani Cahill, who has taught at Goudy for 16 years. "Let me show them how to parent and we wouldn't have the problems we have."

One year, Cahill sent a pre-primer reading book home with 8-year-old twin brothers. Several days had passed and the book had not yet made it back.

So Cahill, one of the few Goudy teachers who tries to narrow the gap between the family and the schoolhouse by making visits to the home, went looking for it.

"I walked into that apartment and I was livid," Cahill recalled. "I demanded to know what happened to that book. The mother told me it was in the bathroom. I said, 'The bathroom?' So I went into the bathroom and found they had torn the pages out and used them as toilet paper. They even showed me how to crumple the pages up and rub them back and forth in their hands to make them soft."

By visiting the homes of many of her students, Cahill said she better understands why they have such a hard time adapting to the structure of school.

"They need mothering more than they need a teacher," Cahill believes.

Cahill has taught lessons about how flowers are for everyone's enjoyment after one of her students went around her classroom and picked all the blooms off her potted plants.

"I passed out dictionaries once to teach a vocabulary lesson," Cahill recalled. "And one of my students started ripping out the pages when he found a word. I said: 'What are you doing? You leave the pages there for the next person.' And he told me: 'That's their problem. This is my word.' So I taught a whole lesson on the value of a book."

But a lot of the time, especially with the children who are the biggest discipline problems, Cahill finds that she does not always get a lot of reinforcement from the home. She has gotten used to that.

One day, she phoned a mother to discuss the volatile temper she was seeing in her son. After she explained the situation, she said the mother made one statement: "I don't know why the f--- you're calling me."

Cahill said she called another mother so many times this year that the mother finally told her not to bother her any more and to call the school social worker instead.

"She kept saying, 'When he goes to jail, I'm not going to come for him,' and I kept trying to say, 'We are not talking about 'when,' we are trying to keep that from happening.

"A lot of these parents," Cahill said, "don't seem to see any options."

"Let's tell the truth here," said teacher Bette Jarrow, who started the

On the home front: *Tugging the arm of her student, Antonio Robertson, to make a point, teacher Fani Cahill discusses discipline with Antonio's mother, Alberta, in a visit to the Robertson home.*

school year with a room of 1st and 2d graders and one 3d grader, most of whom, she said, did not know all of their colors or their numbers. Only a few could read.

"The school has everything but the labor pains," Jarrow said. "A teacher cannot take mom and dad's place. What am I going to accomplish when mom doesn't take the time to pick up a can of peas and say, 'Green! Round! Peas!'?"

'I have to be very careful when I assign homework," teacher David LaRue said of his 4th graders. "I have to make sure it's something we've gone over in class. I can't give them something new because many of the parents either don't help the kids or they don't understand the work the kids bring home."

LaRue, 28, grew up poor in the Robert Taylor Homes public housing project on the South Side. But he had the benefit of a family that expected a lot. Above all, it was intact. He works hard to inspire his 37 students.

"I know the odds are against these children," he explained, "I'm just trying to even them up a little bit."

One of the most haunting discoveries LaRue has made about his students is that already, only midway through grammar school, many of them seem to be losing interest in education.

He sees that their eyes are opening to the world around them, and that many are beginning to understand the realities of the isolated and economically deprived neighborhood they are growing up in. He struggles to translate academics into real-life lessons the children can take with them when they leave his classroom at the end of the school day.

"Sometimes, it's like I'm teaching French," LaRue said.

"These are kids with very little or no self-confidence. Their experience in life has been so limited. They are afraid of learning because it involves something they decide is difficult because it is new.

"These kids are aware of their failures. Some of them act like the game's already over and the other team won.

"And they have to be pushed. They already know they do not have to do a lot of work to get passed on in school."

He knows that a lot of his students are not pushed at home.

He reached in the folder in the bottom drawer of his file cabinet and pulled out a few of the notes that parents have sent to school with their children.

"Christopher has Been absent Last Week Because It was to cold," one of them read.

"Would you please sent Denise home by 12:00 noon Cause I have to go some where and she have no place to go. so if you can give her a pass so she can Leave," another said.

"Gary have a appointment to see the Doctor on friday. I have been going to school. Gary Aunt have been keeping out of school until friday. I think need to be in school."

"Please excuse Tammie for not having her spelling book She let her sister have it she was supposed to have lost it."

LaRue rummaged through a pile of spelling papers until he came up with the paper where "alphabet" was spelled "afeBet," "telephone" was spelled "tellofon," and "enough" was spelled "enof."

Out of the 20 spelling words the children were supposed to study for the test that week, Tammie got only one of them right.

She knew how to spell the month of May.

Even when parents try to do the best for their children, their actions can be touching but counterproductive. Many just don't know how to help the schools help their children.

Ten minutes after the morning bell rang, Marlena Holman walked meekly into Room 210. The 2d grader hung onto the doorknob as she looked at her teacher. It was not an amicable meeting of the eyes.

"Do you have something for me?" teacher Susan Schindler snapped.

Marlena nodded, and handed her a folded up note from home.

Teacher,

Because of an overload of homework Marlena and I was up until 2:30 a.m. on 1-27-88, hence, we overslept yesterday and she was unable to make it to school.

Parent; L. Holman

Then Marlena went to her desk, reached into her bookbag, and pulled out what appeared to be a three-inch stack of homework papers. Schindler couldn't believe her eyes. Marlena had been absent for eight days and the rules of her classroom are that all work must be made up. But not in one day.

"When you owe me work, you know that doesn't mean you give it to me all at once," said Schindler, a dark-haired woman with sharp features who was frowning as she flipped through the pages.

"To get all this done you stayed up

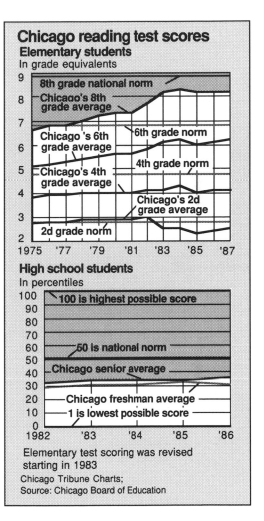

till 2:30 then missed school?"

Marlena nodded.

"Oh, jeez," Schindler said, walking away from the girl and shaking her head.

Mrs. Holman said later at her apartment that she had kept her daughter home because she was sick. Poking her head around her half-open front door, she said also that she felt the schoolwork might be too hard for Marlena.

Schindler, who teaches an accelerated classroom for Goudy's brightest 2d graders, said that Marlena had fallen behind.

"This really frustrates me," said Schindler, "because I care about these children. She can do the work."

Teacher Susan Belter remembers how her classroom was interrupted by a parent who walked to school to complain about the 20-page paper she had assigned on Ancient Egypt to her 6th and 7th graders.

LaKeisha Showers did not turn one in.

"She told me her father said she didn't have to do it, and I said that was not true because that was what I had assigned. Then I look up, and who walks in but LaKeisha's father.

"In front of all the kids, he yells, 'You can't assign that much work to my baby. That's too much for her.' And LaKeisha just sat there and grinned."

Herbert Franklin, LaKeisha's father, explained that he went to school that day and talked to the teacher because his daughter told him she had only one week to do the 20-page paper, and he did not feel that was enough time.

"I told the teacher that was just too much to do in one week," said Franklin, a laid-off die caster.

Asked about his hopes for his daughter, Franklin said he wants her to go to college so she can work as a secretary when she grows up.

Teacher Cahill got tickled one day when she saw one of the boys in her room for children with behavior problems teetering playfully on the inside window ledge. She called him Humpty-Dumpty and she recited the nursery rhyme.

But none of the pre-teen students knew what she meant.

"They thought it was a rap," Cahill remembered. "They had never heard it. They didn't even believe me until I brought in a book of nursery rhymes and pointed to the page and said, 'Look! Here it is!' "

Ann Jardine, a teacher in one of Goudy's remedial 1st-grade classes, remembers the little girl who came to her room at the age of 7 having never spent a day in school.

"Her mother explained that the girl knew her alphabet, and I said, 'Oh?' So she asked the child to sing the alphabet song," Jardine said. "When she was finished, I pointed to some letters on the bulletin board.

"The child had no idea what any of the letters were."

First-grade teacher Helen Harris went to Goudy as a child when the neighborhood was much different. She returned to her public school as a teacher and has been there for 24 years.

But she has still not gotten used to what the children tell her about their family life.

"They talk about fights, knifings, arguments where furniture is thrown and where people are drunk. Many insist there are guns in the house. You really have to step back and think that these are the children you are so desperately trying to teach."

Last year, when Harris found that one of her 1st-grade students had $40, she went to the office and called the parent.

"He said he had just left the store without his cart full of groceries because there was no money in his wallet and I said, 'I know, I've got it right here.' "

The next day, she asked the child what happened.

"Nothing," Harris recalled. "There was no punishment for having stolen money from a parent's wallet."

This year she found one of her 1st graders with $15. She informed the parent, who said the child shouldn't have taken it from home and promised punishment.

The child told Harris the punishment was to watch TV.

"Last year, I was devastated," said Harris. "This year, let's just say I was crucially hurt."

Adapting: By visiting the homes of many of her students, Fani Cahill says she better understands why they have such a hard time adapting to school. "They need mothering more than they need a teacher," she says.

Struggle has reward for 8th grader

For Peaches Barker, 14, the last two years at Bethune Elementary School have been a struggle. Even though she lived through most of one winter in an apartment with no running water and two close family members died—including the grandfather who helped raise her—Peaches managed to improve her scores in reading and arithmetic enough to function in high school.

Her battle is not over. But she's cleared one hurdle. Peaches will graduate from 8th grade in June.

Entering 7th grade, Peaches barely had the reading and math skills of a 4th grader. But she was placed in the room of Corla Hawkins, a robust teacher who is adamant that her children learn.

"I tell them that I ain't training no green card (welfare) club here," said Hawkins, who also kept Peaches in her homeroom for 8th grade at the school at 3030 W. Arthington St.

After 10 months in 7th grade, Peaches had made slightly more than two years' progress in reading and 1½ years' progress in math. In 8th grade, her progress was slower, but she still gained two months in reading and six months in math. She joined the basketball team and Hawkins' after-school drama club.

"I really think I'm going to graduate," Peaches said in February. "Ms. Hawkins cares about us. We study hard for her. Some of the other teachers, if you don't understand something, they just say, 'It's your tough luck.' "

Bethune Principal Warren Franczyk says Peaches will go to high school even though her reading and math scores are two years below grade level.

"Scores aren't everything," Franczyk said. "Her attendance is good, her attitude is good, and she's doing well in her classwork."

In 7th grade, Peaches received a certificate for achievement in reading. Her mother, Diane, went to the award ceremony, and remembers it as "beautiful, all the kids getting their awards."

Study is hard for children like Peaches, who must devote considerable energy to dealing with the pressure in their lives.

Peaches' family lived in an apartment on the West Side for two months this winter with no water. They went to neighbors in the building next door, often in subzero weather, to use the kitchen and bathroom.

"The pipes froze, and the landlord said he was just going to abandon the building," Barker said as she was preparing to move her family of five to a new apartment.

Achiever: Peaches Barker and her mother, Diane, display an award for reading the 8th grader earned last year. Peaches made slightly more than two years' progress in reading during 7th grade.

It took a long time to find a place that Barker, who has been looking for work for five years, could afford on the family's monthly welfare income of $799, including $207 in food stamps.

Barker, 34, was born in Selma, Ala. She remembers the civil rights marches, and believes that they have made a difference for her family.

"We don't have to sit in the back of the bus anymore," Barker said. "We can use any water fountain. All children can go to the same school. We can get the same jobs and the same wages."

Barker says she looks for work nearly every day. She has gone back to school to take typing and word processing.

"It's been five years since I've worked," Barker said. "Today I went to Evanston because I heard there might be jobs at a hospital there. Sometimes I just go downtown and look for help-wanted signs."

In February, after six weeks without water, the smell of dirty diapers filled the small, cramped apartment. It was neat and clean, with worn but tended furniture. The springs no longer worked in the sofa, but there were artificial flowers on the dining room table.

Peaches' older sister, Margaret Jackson, 17, dropped out of high school to have a baby last year, and lives at home. Her brother, Lucky, 16, is a freshman at Manley High School, 2935 W. Polk St.

Peaches, whose real name is Continia, says she enjoyed 8th grade, and has high hopes for the future.

"Some people said Ms. Hawkins wasn't teaching us, because she had us doing a lot of projects," Peaches said. "But she was fooling them. We learned a lot."

"I did a 'say no to drugs' poster, we did science experiments, we had ethnic food days. She makes us want to learn. I want to go to Marshall High School because they have a great girls' basketball team. But I be afraid I'd sit on the bench."

Failing: *Grace Currin has taught her 4th graders so little, her principal says, that all 22 will have to go to summer school in order to move up.*

Tangled supervision
lets inept teachers roam free

'You can recall cars,
you can't recall children'

A ll 22 students in Grace Currin's 4th-grade class must attend summer school this year because, their principal says, Currin did not teach the children enough to pass to the next grade.

"It's a terrible shame," said Dyanne Dandridge-Alexander, principal at Spencer Elementary School. "Those children have suffered because they have a totally inept teacher that no one has been able to fire."

Currin's class—where the principal says she has seen chairs flying across the room—is an extreme example of what thousands of Chicago children face daily: poor teachers, burned-out teachers, teachers who haven't been trained to teach the classes to which they are assigned.

The Chicago Public Schools employ 28,675 teachers. Many are excellent teachers, dedicated and well-trained. But a seven-month examination of the schools by The Tribune also uncovered a disturbing profile of the city's teaching corps, an ingrown, aging workforce of uneven ability.

One out of four is a substitute teacher. Many are in the same class every day, but often without the training or credentials they should have to teach their grade or subject.

Nearly one in five was granted a city teaching certificate even after declining to take, or failing, the exams required of other Chicago teachers.

One in three received a bachelor's degree from one of two local universities. In addition, Chicago teachers are less likely than their suburban counterparts to hold advanced degrees.

The school administration, hamstrung by state law, labor contracts and its own inertia, rarely moves to fire a teacher for incompetence.

Of the 139 teachers who, over the last five years, were so lacking in attendance, discipline, teaching ability or relationships with their students that their principals did try to fire them, 99 are still in Chicago classrooms.

The Chicago Board of Education uses a teaching category called "full-time basis substitute" to sidestep a state law that says teachers must be certified to teach their grade or subject.

Of the 28,675 teachers, 7,294 are substitutes. About 4,350 substitutes teach every day, often assigned to the same class daily, even for a full year.

Many are classified as substitutes because they are not trained for their assignment; a person trained to teach high school but assigned to a 1st-grade room would be classified as a substitute. Other substitutes have not passed the National Teachers Exam or are on a waiting list for a regular position.

For three months this year, none of the substitutes assigned to Du Sable High School's auto shop was a certified auto shop teacher. Uninsured against injury, they could not even touch the cars. Students say that one teacher, assigned to their class for about six weeks, told the students to read their books and slept through many sessions.

Ten weeks into the first semester, typing students at Du Sable, 4934 S. Wabash Ave., had gone through four substitutes, none of them trained to teach typing or certified in any business subject.

During the 11th week, a certified typing teacher arrived, and the students learned where to place their hands on a keyboard. Four weeks later, she took a job in private industry.

The cycle of substitutes began again, only worse. On some days, no teacher showed up at all.

"It's a shame that we have been in this class a whole semester and they still can't find us a teacher," said 15-year-old Tawanda Bradley, who spent most of one teacherless class putting on makeup and fixing her hair. "We'll probably have to take it over again."

Chicago School Supt. Manford Byrd Jr. was surprised that such a situation existed.

"I'm not aware of that kind of imbalance," he said. "Our aim is to get regular certified teachers in all the openings. But I don't know if we've ever been in a better shape than we are now."

At the State Board of Education, Su-

san Bentz, assistant superintendent for teacher certification, was surprised to learn that Chicago uses the substitute category to let people teach full-time in areas where they are not credentialed.

"Technically it's legal, I guess," Bentz said. But, she added, "we would discourage that."

Substitutes are paid less than regular teachers, although Byrd says this has nothing to do with their widespread use.

The substitute pool is also used as a training ground for new teachers. This system batters neophytes through years of other teachers' classrooms.

Beverly Hoover, a certified high school English and math teacher, spent 10 years as a substitute before being assigned to a regular position this year.

"I thought it would be much sooner," said Hoover. "I was even laid off once in 1979, but then I got hired back."

During her four years at Du Sable, Hoover has been robbed twice as she left school, and her desk and supply locker have been burglarized. She now wraps a chain around the locker handle and secures it with an industrial-size lock.

"I would consider other job opportunities," she said.

Manley High School teacher Suzanne Lampka watched recently as two teachers tried to break up a hallway fight between three kicking, scratching girls. Books were flying, and about 50 other students were pushing, shoving and cheering, trying to get close.

"It takes a bold teacher to step in there," says Lampka, brushing a wisp of gray hair off her face. "Most of us are getting too old. There aren't many old, bold teachers."

Lampka is a teacher who spends her own money for supplies for the impoverished students of her all-black school at 2935 W. Polk St., who motivates them to read, who puts a gentle hand on the shoulder of a lanky senior disrupting her class.

She is one of many enthusiastic and skilled women and men who do their jobs well, sometimes heroically.

But their efforts are undermined by those less able or willing to motivate and instruct children.

The Chicago teaching force is an aging one. There are twice as many teachers over 60 years old than under 30. Frequent staff cuts, such as the one that helped pay for the contract that settled last fall's school strike, always hit the youngest teachers.

The average teacher's age is 45, and the Chicago Teachers Union estimates that half the teaching staff may retire within the next decade.

The effects of the aging staff are being seen in higher salaries, greater burnout and less energy.

Among the 99 Chicago teachers who have been recently rated as "unsatisfactory"—a failing grade—the average experience is 19.5 years.

But the graying of the faculty—a phenomenon not unique to Chicago—also is spurring concern that a teacher shortage will develop in city schools. There are fears that the Chicago system is not prepared to address that problem—especially in a competitive market.

"We don't view a possible teacher shortage as a window of opportunity," said CTU Vice President John Kotsakis. "We see it as a danger zone

of lowered standards."

Lowering standards is just what the school board did the last time it faced a critical teacher shortage.

Huge numbers of substitute teachers were hired in the 1960s and 1970s and granted teaching certificates.

Today, at least 4,700 of those teachers remain in classrooms, holding certificates granted between 1968 and 1981—well after the shortage had ended. Many did not take or failed oral exams and the National Teachers Examination, which are required of all other certified Chicago teachers.

"We called them 'gift certificates,' " said Charles Almo, the school board's director of personnel.

Although these teachers comprise 18 percent of the teaching force, they make up 23 percent of teachers whose performance was rated "unsatisfactory" in the past five years.

Principals say these teachers are often good with children but, as Du Sable Principal Judith Steinhagen put it, "I would wish for a little more fluency with the English language."

A lenient administration, a powerful teachers union and a misguided state law have created an environment that protects incompetent teachers and ignores the children they are supposed to teach.

The legal procedure for firing a teacher is protracted, hard-fought and most often unsuccessful. As a result, most principals give passing ratings to all but the most extreme cases.

It is impossible to judge the overall quality of the teaching force by the school bureaucracy's rating scale.

Last year, 70 percent of Chicago

teachers were rated "superior," the highest rating, by their principals; another 20 percent were rated "excellent," according to school records.

That is equivalent to a class with a grading curve so skewed that 9 out of 10 students get A's and B's.

Principals admit that the terms "excellent" and "satisfactory" are misnomers.

Warren Franczyk, principal at Bethune Elementary School, 3030 W. Arthington St., for example, unofficially ranks two of his teachers in the "lowest 20 percent." He calls one "a totally negative person" and the other "indifferent, unable to motivate students."

Yet Franczyk gave both teachers "excellent" ratings last year.

When he gives an "excellent" rating, Franczyk said, "It does not mean this is an excellent teacher.

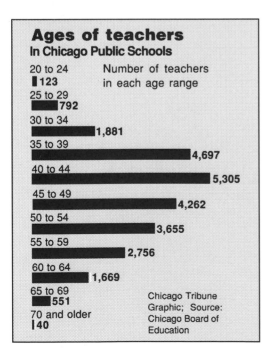

Ages of teachers
In Chicago Public Schools

Age range	Number of teachers in each age range
20 to 24	123
25 to 29	792
30 to 34	1,881
35 to 39	4,697
40 to 44	5,305
45 to 49	4,262
50 to 54	3,655
55 to 59	2,756
60 to 64	1,669
65 to 69	551
70 and older	40

Chicago Tribune Graphic; Source: Chicago Board of Education

"It means they are falling short on something—teaching proficiency, attendance, attitude towards children or relationships with parents.

"I haven't given an 'unsatisfactory' for a long time," he said. "You have to prove gross negligence. The process is too long."

Many principals say they allow bad teachers to stay rather than go through the arduous firing procedures and then face a team of union attorneys in a lengthy dismissal hearing.

"A teacher has to be really bad—I mean terrible—before most principals will bother to go through the firing process," said school board attorney Denise Cahill.

Or principals simply trade a bad teacher to another school, in the hope that a new setting will cure the burnout, improve the attitude or somehow jog forgotten skills.

"It is a situation where a principal says, 'I'll take your bad apple if you'll take mine,'" said Powhatan Collins, principal of Whitney Young Magnet School, 211 S. Laflin St.

School officials can remove poor teachers from the classroom, but they seldom do. They need to gather evidence to build a case against a teacher. But a stronger motivation is simple economics.

"You would have that person sitting on the cooler being paid when you need services in the classroom," said Byrd. "You're adding to your payroll in a nonproductive way."

But educators insist that different criteria must be used.

"Teachers are not like factory workers where the boss can recall a product if someone puts a bolt or a lug nut on the wrong way," said Stephen Horowitz, assistant principal at Maria Saucedo Magnet Elementary School, 2850 W. 24th Street Blvd.

"You can recall cars, but you can't recall children. This is their only shot at an education."

Even when a teacher is judged unsatisfactory, there is little likelihood that he or she will be removed from the classroom. Failing teachers can slip quietly through the system, moving from school to school, for years.

Consider the case of Grace Currin.

Four principals have tried unsuccessfully to fire Currin. Because of her inability in the classroom, her current principal says, Currin's entire 4th-grade class at Spencer Elementary School, 214 N. Lavergne Ave., will have to go to summer school to have any hope of making it to 5th grade in September.

"It is really a joke that the system allows this to happen," said Spencer Principal Dyanne Dandridge-Alexander. "Those children deserve a better teacher, a better education."

Currin, 56, has taught for 30 years and is paid $35,489. No record of her ratings is available before 1966, but she received 12 "excellent" ratings and 5 "superior" ratings between 1966 and 1983.

In the 1983-1984 school year, Currin received her first "unsatisfactory" rating, at Fermi Elementary School, 1415 E. 70th St.

Her second came during the next year at Oakenwald Elementary, 4061 S. Lake Park Ave. She improved to "satisfactory" in 1985-86 but received a third "unsatisfactory" at Douglass Middle

School, 543 N. Waller Ave., in 1987, according to records. Dandridge-Alexander gave her a fourth this March.

Robert Saddler, the local district superintendent, said he "didn't bother" to look at Currin's file, which contained the negative ratings, before he transferred her to Spencer.

"I didn't feel the need to call up and get her work record," Saddler said.

Currin "has not handed in a lesson plan all year," Dandridge-Alexander said, "and when you ask her about it she says, 'I left it at home.'

"The noise level in the class is unbelievable. Kids are fighting. Children are rolling around on the floor. They are throwing chairs across the room. One day I walked into her classroom and said, 'Did you see that chair fly across the room?' and she said, 'I told them not to do that.' "

Dandridge-Alexander called parents in April and asked them to sit in on Currin's classes. In May, the principal asked parents how things were going. "They are at a point where they think it is hopeless," she said.

Currin says she does not deserve the negative ratings.

"I still think they did not really get to know me as a teacher," she said. "I am part of the problem, but remember, you can't expect miracles when you have low achievers. There always will be discipline problems in that class. It's the kind of children that I teach."

Currin, who said her career goal is "to retire at full pension," declined to comment further on her classroom performance, saying: "I have to make sure that I will be able to work a little while longer. This [conversation] will keep me from progressing to the next highest attainment that I want to do."

Grace Currin will be able to continue teaching until at least March, 1989, under a new state law that gives unsatisfactory teachers a full year to work before they can be dismissed.

"What if she doesn't improve by the time the next school year starts?" Dandridge-Alexander said. "Another class of children might lose a year of their education."

The new law, ironically a part of the 1985 state school reform package, extended to one year from 45 days the time that poor teachers have to improve. It also provides them a consulting teacher.

Although the measure was drafted by school management as a strengthened tool to weed out weak teachers, lobbying by teachers unions turned it into a law that made it even more difficult to fire teachers.

Union officials defend the law, saying it promotes a "spirit of collegiality and teamwork."

"This might help by providing advice and support," said Chicago Teachers Union President Jacqueline Vaughn. "And it gives our more experienced teachers recognition."

The board is pushing legislation to reduce the time a poor teacher has with a consulting teacher to 50 days from one year, but Vaughn called that proposal "dangerous" and "a power grab."

Union officials deny that the union protects incompetents and say that school officials are too lazy to monitor teachers.

Unsatisfactory teaching wasn't enough to get James Rayford Hall III out of the classroom.

Three principals initiated the process to fire Hall for poor classroom performance between 1978 and 1986. But he was not suspended from teaching until he was arrested and charged with sexually abusing two male students.

Hall taught in 15 Chicago schools in 18 years. At no time until his arrest was there evidence of suspected child abuse.

But principals tried unsuccessfully to fire Hall for classroom incompetence at Mather High School, 5835 N. Lincoln Ave., in 1978 and at Lake View High School, 4015 N. Ashland Ave., in 1980.

In the 1982-83 school year, Hall took a leave of absence and taught in Dallas, where he was fired for incompetence, according to evidence later entered in a Chicago hearing.

Chicago officials reinstated Hall in 1983. But the principal at Chicago Vocational High School, 2100 E. 87th St., gave him another unsatisfactory notice for tardiness and other classroom problems in April, 1986.

On Sept. 26, 1986, Hall was arrested on charges of aggravated criminal sexual assault on two 15-year-old male students. He pleaded innocent and is awaiting trial.

He was taken out of the classroom that October and worked in a district office until January, 1987, when he was officially suspended and the school board moved to fire him.

A hearing was held this February on the bid to dismiss Hall, who told the hearing officer he would like to return to teaching. A decision is expected this summer.

"This is someone who probably should have been booted out of the system a long time ago," said Camille Willis, a board attorney handling the case. "But he kept landing on his feet until the board had no choice but to suspend him after criminal charges were filed."

Hearing officers are chosen from a list compiled by the State Board of Education. By state law, they must live outside the involved district. They are often university professors or lawyers, and board attorneys say they are frequently unfamiliar with the problems of a large urban school system.

Willis is cautiously optimistic that she will not see Hall back in a classroom. But she and other board attorneys have seen hearing officers subvert their efforts to fire teachers before.

Willie Box, then a 5th-grade teacher at Yates Elementary School, 1839 N. Richmond St., was suspended and charged with sexual misconduct in 1986 after five girls said Box had fondled them in class.

At his dismissal hearing, two other students said they had seen it happen. Both his principal and district superintendent testified they had warned Box about his behavior.

Box stated that he touched students "only in the normal course of day-to-day activities" and denied touching any in inappropriate areas.

The hearing officer, Chicago lawyer Peter R. Meyers, said he was "convinced that many of the episodes of physical contact were not proper," but he ruled against firing Box because "school administrators did not hold any workshops on the subject of physical contact between students and teachers."

The board appealed, and a Circuit Court judge last November sent the case back to the hearing officer, saying

the original ruling was "contrary to law." Box remains suspended from teaching.

Teacher Deborah Harris was suspended from Shoop Elementary School, 1460 W. 112th St., after she consistently refused to go to her 7th-grade classroom. Each day she gave the principal a doctor's note saying that she should be given "light duties," according to statements presented during her dismissal hearing in 1986.

Harris was told daily, in writing, by the principal and the district superintendent to report to class. She hid in the boiler room, according to testimony.

The hearing officer, Marvin Hill, a law professor at Northern Illinois

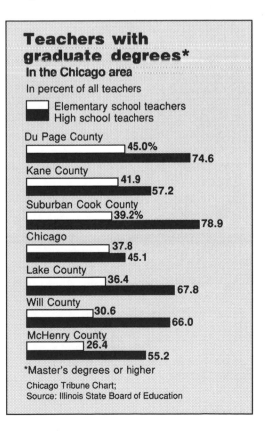

Teachers with graduate degrees*
In the Chicago area
In percent of all teachers

☐ Elementary school teachers
■ High school teachers

Du Page County
45.0%
74.6

Kane County
41.9
57.2

Suburban Cook County
39.2%
78.9

Chicago
37.8
45.1

Lake County
36.4
67.8

Will County
30.6
66.0

McHenry County
26.4
55.2

*Master's degrees or higher
Chicago Tribune Chart;
Source: Illinois State Board of Education

University, ordered Harris reinstated because the board had not given her written notice that she would be fired if she did not go to class.

Harris took a leave of absence last Dec. 7, the day she was reinstated to Curtis Elementary School, 32 E. 115th St., and has not yet returned.

The board appealed the ruling but lost.

"We were shocked," attorney Cahill said. "Hearing officers view this as a man's or a woman's livelihood. The hearing officer barely mentioned the children."

Incompetent or abusive teachers make up only a small part of the Chicago Public Schools faculty.

But several trends have come together over the past three decades to lower the quality of Chicago's teaching staff, a group assigned the critical chore of teaching some of the nation's most impoverished and troubled children.

Chicago teachers' salaries—which average $31,058 and range from $17,156 for a beginner with a bachelor's degree to $36,465 for a 15-year veteran with a Ph.D.—are determined solely by years on the job and education level.

Their salaries, once among the highest in the state, now come within a few hundred dollars of the local suburban average and are considerably lower than salaries paid to most suburban high school teachers.

There is no financial incentive in the Chicago union contract to reward top-notch teaching and superlative effort— except to leave the classroom for a higher-paying administrative job.

Chicago teachers also are discouraged from furthering their own education by a salary schedule that holds little reward for advanced degrees. And Chicago, unlike nearly half of Illinois school districts, does not reimburse tuition costs.

Forty-five percent of Chicago high school teachers have master's degrees, compared with 78.9 percent in suburban Cook County. Chicago grade school teachers are also less likely to have advanced degrees than their suburban counterparts, but the gap is narrower.

For Chicago teachers with only bachelor's degrees, the difference between a beginner's salary and that of a teacher with 15 years' experience—the top longevity step—is $15,407.

But a veteran teacher who takes the time and expense to earn master's and doctoral degrees gains only $3,902. By contrast, most suburban districts do not allow a teacher, especially a high school teacher, to advance in salary beyond a certain point without going back to school.

Nearly $22,700 separates the top salary available to a Niles High School District 219 teacher with a bachelor's degree from the top salary of a colleague with an advanced degree. Niles teachers with bachelor's degrees must go back to school after eight years to get more money.

Chicago school bureaucrats do not see the dearth of advanced degrees among their teachers as a problem.

"It is nice to say that people with more education do a better job," said Michael Wrenn, director of the board's bureau of employee relations and a negotiator in labor contract talks.

"But I'm not sure that's true. When I came in, a lot of the teachers only had two years of normal school. I went to Catholic school, and a lot of the nuns didn't even have a college degree.

"I think the most important thing for an elementary teacher is the love of children," Wrenn said. "Give them the bachelor's degree, and then if they need another art course or something, they'll go and get it."

Principals disagree.

"I can really see the difference when teachers have advanced degrees and take courses to stay current in their field," said Collins, principal of Whitney Young.

"It boosts their self-esteem," Collins said. "They become more professional. Their skills improve, and their accomplishments raise the intellectual ability of the total school."

Chicago schools also have difficulty attracting teachers from beyond their own boundaries. Thousands of city teachers graduated from Chicago public schools, went to local colleges and cycled back into the city schools.

More than one-third of the teachers received their bachelor's degrees from Chicago State University and Northeastern Illinois University, two colleges whose students come primarily from the Chicago area. Incoming freshmen at each school have average ACT scores of 15, compared with the average of 18.9 for all Illinois high school seniors.

School administrators seem complacent about the present and future quality of the Chicago teaching force and whether they can meet the needs of Chicago schoolchildren.

"We are recruiting all the time," Almo said. "It will be interesting to see if a lot of teachers retire soon. Principals let us know what their needs are."

Neither Charles Almo, school board director of personnel, nor Raymond Principe, director of teacher personnel, could name any specific plans to deal with the predicted teacher shortage, to lessen the reliance on uncertified substitutes or to retain qualified teachers.

But promising college education majors are being steered elsewhere.

C.C. Mitchell, a Chicago teacher who testified during state Senate hearings last fall, said the reputation of Chicago schools has spread to area colleges.

"The word is out to student teachers," Mitchell said. " 'Do not get involved with Chicago Public Schools.' "

Michael Bakalis, dean of Loyola University's school of education and a former state school superintendent, said frequent strikes and a "reputation as being overcentralized and overbureaucracized" hurt Chicago schools in competing for teachers.

"Teachers are better prepared than ever and want some sense of involvement and creativity," Bakalis said. "They don't want to be stifled at every turn by bureaucratic rules or worry about being out of work every other year.

"The job opportunities over the next 10 years in teaching will be tremendous with the aging population of teachers. There will be a buyer's market, and you have to wonder why people would come to Chicago."

Learning is fun: *Bethune teacher Corla Hawkins runs a drama club for about 40 students. Her strength lies in her ability to motivate and love and nurture the needy children in her charge.*

Any reason is good reason for a 'Mrs. Hawk' lesson

'You will not fail, do you hear me?'

Corla Hawkins is padding around Room 300 in her house slippers, singing "The Lord is My Shepherd," trying to be teacher-mother-bully-counselor to a room full of children no one else wants to teach—the slowest 7th and 8th graders in Bethune Elementary School.

When the children's test scores say they can't read, Hawkins has them memorize poems and act out plays.

When one girl shows up pregnant, the class does a project on ultrasound.

When one-third of the class has no mittens, Hawkins brings in her sewing machine and teaches the children to make mittens from old sweaters.

"My dream is to have a whole house full of really needy kids and do great things with them," says Hawkins, who has taught at Bethune, 3030 W. Arthington St., since 1986.

It is late in the day, and Hawkins has heard from another teacher that her homeroom students have failed a spelling test. Another test is scheduled tomorrow.

"Pair up, everyone of you," she says. "You call each other tonight and drill those spelling words. Those who don't have a phone, go to each other's houses. I will give you the test at 9 a.m. tomorrow, and you'll be ready. You will not fail, do you hear me? You will not fail."

Hawkins is not the most academically gifted teacher—she once told the children to call brain surgeons to see how many people had gotten tumors from hair permanents—but her strength lies in her ability to motivate children, to make them want to learn, to love and nurture the needy children in her charge.

A former student, Jamal Cheeks, wrote this message on a graduation poster that Hawkins' 8th graders made last June: "My mother was having a fit about me possibly failing. But Mrs. Hawk scared the dust off my brains and I passed, I did, I did!"

Tatanisha Parks came to Hawkins from a private school in 7th grade with test scores showing 2d-grade reading skills and 3d-grade math skills.

Working hard—and backed up her parents—she pushed her scores to mid-9th grade in two years.

"We expect a lot of 'Ta'," said Albert Parks, a Chicago policeman, using his daughter's nickname.

Ta's mother, Raven Parks, gives Hawkins much of the credit: "She really cares about those kids, and so many of them are lost kids. They have nothing."

Hawkins is paid $24,153. A former high school teacher, she was certified as an elementary teacher in February after six years as a full-time grade school substitute.

"Her methods are unorthodox, but I see happy, productive children in her room who are learning," said Bethune Principal Warren Franczyk.

Bethune's students come from one of the city's poorest areas.

Hawkins spends as much time talking about life as about academics. On one day, class members—both boys and girls—talked about what they would do if they were raped, how they would feel, who they would tell.

Being homeroom teacher to the lowest 7th and 8th grade means Hawkins often has to tell her students things they do not want to hear.

Today the bad news is that the other 8th grades have decided they will dress in white dresses and suits for graduation ceremonies, rather than caps and gowns.

"For our graduation? For our graduation?" screams Peaches Barker. "I'm not coming. I want to wear caps and gowns like everybody else."

"Let me tell you a secret," Hawkins says. "If you're not reading in the 8th-grade book, if your test scores aren't what they should be, you're not supposed to graduate.

"I can fight for you to graduate or I can fight for caps and gowns. I'm not going to take no hard way to go. Now, what is it going to be? Caps and gowns or coming out of here in June?"

Scattered mutters are heard from around the room. "Come out of here in June."

It is five minutes before the end of the day, and in the other rooms on the third floor, the children have packed their books. But there is still teaching to be done in Room 300—a 3-sentence paragraph in the composition books.

When the students finish, the day ends as it usually does in Hawkins' room. "Very good," she says. "I'm very proud of you. I love you all. See you tomorrow."

And her students respond: "Thank you, Miz Hawkins!"

Labor of love: *"My dream is to have a whole house full of really needy kids and do great things with them," says Hawkins.*

Deserving students get a teacher they deserve

It's 5:30 a.m. and Thomas Kling has already hit the road on the long journey from his North Shore home to the Douglass Middle School on the West Side.

Kling, a Chicago public school teacher for 13 years, pulls into the parking lot at Douglass, 543 N. Waller Ave., about 6:15 a.m., and slips in a back door with some lunchroom employees who start work long before the school doors officially open at 8 a.m.

He makes his way through the dark, abandoned corridors to room 312, where he can work without interruption for two hours before his 29 8th graders spill into the classroom at 8:55 a.m. for the start of the school day.

"I guess you could call it dedication," Kling says as he stands in a classroom with stained carpet, tattered curtains and a climate that fluctuates from stifling heat to shivering cold. "The kids deserve so much and the system gives them so little. There's barely enough time in the day to give them everything that they need."

Kling is the kind of teacher whose skill, dedication and energy far exceed what is expected.

One day about three years ago Kling stood in front of his class of black children and realized that Dick-and-Jane-type textbooks were "about as foreign as Arabic" to his students, many of whom come from poor homes in rough neighborhoods.

"I knew those books would never reach these children, never make them excited enough to pick up a book and read it cover to cover," Kling said.

So he decided to stray from the prescribed curriculum and spice his reading list with books closer to the experience and culture of his students.

"Frankly, the materials that we have to work with are so damn boring," Kling said. "I just feel a lot better coming in every day to school knowing that I can present things that I find relevant and challenging."

Brian Hill, 14, said Kling's emphasis on reading has changed his life.

"I never liked to read until Mr. Kling showed me that reading can be fun." Brian said. "If he could follow me all through high school, I'd be happy."

Kling's reading list includes several works that deal with race and class issues, books he buys with his own money from used-book stores and off-price catalogues. By his tally, he has spent more than $3,000 in the last three years, and he never asks the students to give the books back.

This fall, 32 copies of a book he ordered about growing up under apartheid in South Africa were lost between a New York publisher's warehouse and the Chicago Board of Education headquarters.

"I could have let it go and let the students read something else," Kling said. "But I thought it was important for them to learn about life in South Africa."

Important enough for Kling to visit more than a dozen bookstores to scrape together a set of 32 books at $8.95 each.

"I'm not a rich man, but it's worth it," said Kling, who earns $31,890 a year. "Cost is no objective if I can get my students to read."

And he has, to the extent that he sometimes has a hard time getting them

Energetic: "I feel better knowing that I can present things that I find relevant and challenging," Thomas Kling says.

to concentrate on regular subjects.

Kenneth Crowder, 14, sat in the back of the class one day with his forehead resting on his desktop, his eyes cast down at a book called "Singin' and Swingin' and Gettin' Merry Like Christmas."

Halfway across the room, Diedre Brown, 14, was secretly reading a copy of another book placed inside the open pages of her math book.

Kling, lecturing in front of the class, spotted Crowder, head down, in the back of the room.

"C'mon, you guys," Kling said, "I know you all want to read, but there is plenty of time for that after school."

Though the books Kling buys are sometimes a distraction, he says they have helped to stir the students' appetite for knowledge and have prompted many to work harder at other subjects.

"Teachers used to treat me like I was stupid, like I could never be smart," said Elroy Leach, 13, whose reading scores jumped five grade levels in the three years in Kling's classes. "Mr. Kling isn't like that. He believes that every child is smart in his own way."

Kling has done more than just teach his students how to read, said Douglass Principal Alvin Lubov:

"He has taught those students how to enjoy reading, and that is something that will forever change their lives. I would put my child in that class, and that is the highest praise that I can give a teacher."

Worth the price: *Students at Douglass Middle School read books paid for by Thomas Kling, who scraped together a set of 32 books at $8.95 each.*

Show of force: *Teachers display their dislike for administrators' salaries at a rally in the Daley Center plaza during last fall's strike.*

Teachers union
clamps its vise on the system

'I don't care about you
unless I'm paid.'

T he Chicago Teachers Union has emerged over the past two decades as the most powerful single force in the Chicago public school system.
The muscle comes from an unusually pervasive contract that extends the union's reach into areas of operations and policy reserved for management in almost every kind of labor contract.

This gives the CTU as much control over operations of the public schools as the Chicago Board of Education and School Supt. Manford Byrd Jr. It gives the union more control than is available to principals, parents, taxpayers, voters and business leaders.

It is backed up by clout in Springfield, where the laws on education and collective bargaining are made, as well as the traditional union ability to shut down "the company" by strike when contract demands are not met.

"The CTU has been granted a much greater role in shaping school policies than have teacher unions elsewhere in the state," said R. Theodore Clark Jr., an attorney with Seyfarth, Shaw, Fairweather and Geraldson.

"From a management standpoint, the language in the contract is not very good," said Clark, whose law firm is the largest in the nation specializing in representing management in labor matters. "It limits the ability of the board to implement and affect day-to-day policy."

Veteran labor lawyer Sherman Carmell, who represents the Chicago Federation of Labor and many other local unions, including the Teamsters, calls the CTU contract "one of the most comprehensive I have ever seen.

"The union has actually taken the role of co-manager," said Carmell, of Carmell, Charone, Widmer and Mathews Ltd.

"That has weakened management considerably. For the union, this is a very good contract."

The CTU is Local 1 of the American Federation of Teachers, an AFL-CIO affiliate, because in 1916 it became the first local chapter in the nation to be chartered by the AFT.

Many contract provisions considered onerous by administrators date back to bargaining for the original contract in 1967, when school negotiators were less sophisticated.

"You get the sense from this contract that is the product of people who, over the years, have determined that they don't trust each other," Carmell said.

"This is what we call a 'bright line' contract. Everything is spelled out—'This is all you can require me to do.' Everybody knows when they can hunker down and stand on their rights."

The many rules set by the contract hamstring the education of Chicago's 419,537 students:

• The pact includes a grievance definition so broad that teachers can file a formal complaint about almost anything, restricting management's ability to alter day-to-day school operations.

A grievance can be anything that is a change from a past practice or policy. Even curriculum matters, such as the program for teaching children to read, are written into the contract, requiring the board to bring any proposed changes to the bargaining table.

In California, by contrast, a state law specifically excludes curriculum from collective bargaining. The grievance definition in New York City's school contract is narrower than Chicago's.

• Rules for hiring, firing, transferring and evaluating teachers are so cumbersome that they have eviscerated the power of the local principal to choose and assign staff.

• The contract is so generous in granting sick leaves—and so strict on holding jobs for teachers on leave—that the board has to employ an unusually large number of substitute teachers and frequently bounce them through classes for which they are untrained.

"There are three dozen different places that teachers or union representatives are granted time off with pay and with substitutes," said Clark, who along with Carmell and others, analyzed the CTU contract at the request of The Tribune.

"It is a very real question whether all the paid, nonteaching time can be justified, especially when you think about what happens to the children," Clark said.

But the union says that while the contract does benefit teachers, it is a case of enlightened self-interest: What helps teachers also helps students.

"The children will naturally benefit if we improve the quality of the profession," CTU President Jacqueline Vaughn said in an interview. "It is the teachers who are responsible for teaching the children."

Vaughn recently told teachers at Philip H. Sheridan Elementary, 9000 S. Exchange Ave.: "I resent your efforts being taken for granted and [people] saying we are responsible for the ills in education because, without us, they would have none."

Only part of the union's power has come from its own efforts. A great deal has been ceded to it over the years by a school administration too weak and too strapped for money to hold its own.

The board "is constantly reacting to the union" and has no "long-term plan for changes in the contract," said former school board President George Munoz.

"If the board ever had any money, it could say, 'We might be able to do this for you, but we want to modify this grievance procedure or make it easier to get rid of incompetent teachers.'

"But it is always asking the union to settle for no raises. It would be a joke, counterproductive, for the board to try to get changes along with having no money. You can't do that."

Labor lawyer Carmell said the specificity of the Chicago contract—especially in class size, number of substitutes, even the architecture of certain classrooms—is unusual among modern labor pacts.

"Only in the days of the old craft unions would you have seen the number of people needed to produce a certain number of widgets spelled out so clearly," he said.

Vaughn says the union must be that specific, or the board will take advantage of teachers.

"There may be teachers who will abuse the contract, but they are few," she contends. "The details are in there because if we don't spell it out, the board won't do it.

"You would not believe the months we spent arguing that teachers, teacher aides and school clerks needed a 10-minute bathroom break in the morning and one in the afternoon."

The contract, for instance, spells out that "each school shall provide a desk, a chair and a file cabinet for the school nurse . . . a desk, a chair and a space for the wraps of the truant officer."

It also states that new art rooms shall have "adequate lighting, sinks and cabinets for storage space," and that in buildings more than 10 years old, high school music rooms "shall be surveyed for rehabilitation."

Teachers can be gone for up to 25 months—2½ school years—with paid medical benefits and return to a guaranteed job. During the first 10 months, they can be replaced only by substitutes, not regular teachers.

In March, for example, 704 teachers were on sick leave, 283 were on maternity leave and 36 were on study or special leaves.

Teachers also can save up to 244 sick days, take a sick leave just before retirement and get paid the entire amount. If they cash in unused sick days at retirement, they get just half of the value.

More than 200 teachers have retired straight out of sick leaves in the past five years. In response to complaints by board member Winnie Slusser, school officials are trying to determine the cost of this practice.

"When people retire or resign out of a sick leave, their class is covered by a sub, even if they have no intention of coming back," Slusser said.

"People abuse the things that allow them to get by with as little as possible and, in this case, the abuse is hurting the system."

Teachers who are about to receive "unsatisfactory"—failing—notices sometimes take sick leave before the principal can fill out the forms to begin the process to fire them. This is totally within the rules.

Waymon Jones went to Douglass Middle School, 543 N. Waller Ave., as a science teacher after post-strike budget cuts last fall bumped him from his job as district coordinator.

After only a few weeks, Douglass Principal Alvin Lubov says, he gave Jones a warning that his classroom performance was unsatisfactory and began the procedure required to fire him.

Jones took a sick leave less than a week before the final visit required of the principal and district superintendent to give him an unsatisfactory rating.

If Jones returns and transfers to another school, he could start with a clean slate. Jones' salary when he went on leave was $36,465.

Labor attorney Carmell said that many current contract provisions are a reaction to arbitrary treatment by school boards and administrators.

Especially in the evaluation process, Carmell said, teachers have fought for objective methods of judging their performance.

"That way, a principal can't say, 'You did great on your orals and your written, but I just don't think you'll fit in,' he said. "What they might be saying is, 'You don't fit as well as my brother-in-law's wife who wants the job.'

"They have succeeded more than most public employees in making the evaluation process objective," Carmell said. "They have done a good job of professionalizing their profession."

Carmell called the complaint by principals that the firing process is too cumbersome "a cop-out."

"The process may be cumbersome, but you are talking about someone's livelihood."

Richard Tygielski, the board's chief negotiator, acknowledged that much of the evaluation process was set up by the board.

"It was set up to remediate poor teachers," Tygielski said. "That was the most important. It also makes sure that all the proper procedures were followed so that you had developed your case and a judge could not throw it out."

In some suburban districts, school boards have been able to win contract provisions requiring teachers to donate a certain number of preparation periods or other time to help fill in for sick teachers.

The absence of such a provision in Chicago translates into the need for a large pool of substitute teachers, but the board cannot find enough to meet the demand. On an average day in Chicago schools, 190 classes and 5,700 students are without a teacher.

The teachers' contract, and the way the board administers it, also disrupt children's lives through an almost constant process called "bumping."

Because of seniority provisions, the elimination of just one position held by a person with a teaching certificate—even working in the central office—might affect dozens of teachers and hundreds of students. This is due to the trickle-down process that occurs as those with more experience take the classrooms of those with less, until the newest teachers are pushed out of work or into the substitute pool.

Hundreds of new teachers are hired and full-time substitutes are given regular teaching assignments after the first semester each year, triggering a ripple of midyear staff adjustments. In February, 154 new teachers were hired and 38 substitutes were given new classrooms, meaning that at least 5,760 children got new teachers at midyear.

On Sept. 28, 1987, during the ninth Chicago teachers strike in 19 years, Charlene Kopnick crossed a picket line to report to her district office.

Twenty picketers, including a leader with a bullhorn, chanted, "Charlene Kopnick is a scab," according to a complaint Kopnick filed with the Illinois Educational Labor Relations Board. Her complaint, which asked that the union be dissolved, was denied.

The next day, says Kopnick, a public school teacher since 1964, her car was blocked and hit by a CTU organizer as she drove into the parking lot.

"I hadn't worked since June, and I needed the money," Kopnick said. "But I also didn't think we should be on strike. I used to be a militant unionist, but I resigned from the CTU a few years ago.

"The union has become a powerful bureaucracy that is insensitive to people," she said. "It doesn't care about children.

"I'd like to make more money, but until we can give people the right kind of return on their tax dollars, we don't deserve a raise."

Kopnick, who teaches 5th grade at Plamondon Elementary, 1525 S. Wash-

tenaw Ave., is in the minority among Chicago teachers.

The vast majority belong to the Chicago Teachers Union. It's 28,000 members include teachers, assistant principals, school nurses, librarians, social workers, psychologists, counselors, truant officers, hearing testers, vision testers, library assistants, clerks, teacher aides, school aides, instructional aides, interpreter aides, interpreter clerks and community representatives.

Members pay $346 a year in dues, deducted from their paychecks. Workers who choose not to join the union pay 85 percent of that, or $294.

A copy of the current union budget, which the union says it sent to the Tribune, was never received, and union spokesman Chuck Burdeen said he was

Word from the boss: Teachers at Bowen High on the South Side listen to a speech by Jacqueline Vaughn. She has said that the union must be specific in the contract or the board will take advantage of teachers.

unable to find another copy.

The CTU's 1983 federal income tax forms, the most recent available, showed annual revenue of $5.6 million and annual expenses of $5.8 million.

The union's power is implemented in each school through a delegate and a professional problems committee made up of the delegate and other CTU members.

The committee is encouraged to meet at least once a month with the principal "to discuss school operations and questions," according to the 1987 CTU's delegate's handbook of policies and procedures.

Issues that can be discussed include discipline, staffing, working conditions and educational policy, according to the handbook.

Union delegates are advised, when meeting with the principal, to: "Remember that this is a meeting of equals. You and the other members of the professional problems committee are acting as official representatives of the Chicago Teachers Union, not merely as faculty members under the principal's supervision."

The school board negotiates with 17 other unions, which with the CTU represent 90 percent of the 41,389 employees.

A 1983 agreement in which the CTU and the other unions agreed to respect each others' strikes, and to remain out until everyone was satisfied, has held through four strikes.

"That was the turning point, when the teachers union really became part of the labor movement in Chicago," said Carmell.

"In the 1984 strike, [then-Supt.] Ruth Love had fired two supervising engi-neers for refusing to cross the picket line. The engineers refused to go back until the men were reinstated," Carmell said. "The teachers stood with them, and the strike went on another day, until 3 a.m., when Love realized they were serious.

"That was when the teachers recognized that they were workers, that their interests lie with the carpenters, truck drivers and engineers in their schools."

With nearly all the workforce unionized and united, Vaughn has the leverage she has needed to win pay raises and beneficial contract provisions, and to build a spirit of union solidarity.

There was a time when Vaughn would walk into a union rally, always fashionably late, and the audience would erupt into shouts of "Jacqui! Jacqui! Jacqui!"

But her popularity waned in the settlement of the bitter 19-day strike last fall. The walkout jolted parents into unprecedented protests and resulted in a new contract that gave teachers a 4 percent raise.

Teachers won a raise in a two-year contract contingent upon new money being available for the second year. It also won a reduction in average class size in a few schools. But Vaughn was criticized by many union members for accepting a small raise that was funded in part by eliminating positions. The contract was approved by the closest ballot in CTU history.

Deborah Underwood, a 7th-grade teacher at Piccolo Elementary, 1040 N. Keeler Ave., crossed the picket line during the 1985 and 1987 strikes because, she said, "It's like saying [to the children], 'I don't care about you unless I'm getting paid.' "

Despite last fall's strike, Vaughn had

only one challenger when she ran for re-election, and the opponent, George Schmidt, an English teacher at Amundsen High, is a longtime union dissident.

Vaughn contends that the narrow contract approval was more a show of anger toward the Board of Education than a statement against the CTU and its leadership.

"The members are not angry at me or the union," Vaughn said. "They are angry that they had to walk the picket line for four weeks to get a raise that the board could have afforded all along. I think I've done a good job, and I think the members know that, too."

The changing attitude of some members, however, was evident during a union meeting in February. The CTU president was greeted with only a scattering of applause, and more than half the audience left early.

And Vaughn's suggestion that the union newspaper include columns from other unions such as the Teamsters, as a way of forming a caucus, elicited hisses.

"The CTU is like a family to us," one man yelled. "I suggest you consider that. If you want to run for political office, do it outside of the union."

Labor negotiations are traditionally held behind closed doors. What plays out publicly tends to be posturing. In bigtime negotiations, especially in the public sector, it is critical for each side to seek public sympathy.

During Chicago teacher strikes, television appearances by union and board representatives are choreographed. Major announcements are timed to gibe with the evening television news.

It was public dissatisfaction with both sides that finally forced a settlement of last fall's strike. When that dissatisfaction reached Mayor Harold Washington, he told the 11 men and women he had appointed to run the schools that it was time to throw in the towel, according to Munoz.

"After 19 days, the mayor told the board that he felt that the children's interests were becoming subservient to what had clearly become a personal battleground," Munoz said.

Four months later, with the public still clamoring for reform, several key players were asked about the strike.

"There's a missing piece of the puzzle that I'm not sure anyone can find," said Munoz.

"Vaughn could not accept a contract with cutbacks. We knew that. But she had several alternatives . . . [but] she went on strike, betting completely that a third party would intervene in the strike. She took that risk, and she lost."

Vaughn sees the situation differently.

"Some people overplayed their hand," Vaughn said. "The board was operating under the assumption that money would be forthcoming. The mayor said he had enough votes to override [Gov. James] Thompson's veto.

"My members remembered two years before when we went back without a contract and then had to go traipsing out in December, on the coldest day of the year. They told me, 'Never again.'

"So there we were, looking like fools, wagging around with our sticks when every other district in the state was in school. And at the same time, our brother and sister locals around the nation were getting big raises."

One board member who has lived through several strikes says that the familar steps signaling the end of a strike didn't occur this time.

Ironically, he said, the usual procedure involves an outside labor leader or politician playing the role that the public thinks mediators get paid to do.

"We'll get a call from Bob Healey [former CTU president, now president of the Chicago Federation of Labor] or from the mayor or the governor.

"Healey will call and say, 'I know this is what you've offered, but Jacqui will never take it. Are you sure you can't come up with something better?' And you have to be straight with him because you need him to put the screws to Jacqui when he is sure that you've made your final offer.

"When he is sure that you have nothing more to give, he plays the same game with Jacqui. After awhile, Healey will tell Jacqui, 'That's all you're going to get. Get your people in.'

"This time, this didn't happen," the board member said. "No one came to close the deal."

Instead, the settlement echoed the times when the late Mayor Richard J. Daley would stride into negotiations and tell the board to give the teachers a raise—whether the money was there or not.

Vaughn blames Supt. Manford Byrd Jr. for the breakdown in the bargaining process.

"I have nothing bad to say about the board's negotiating team," she said. "But when it got to the money, they were just a shell. You hear me? Byrd would not allow his team to make decisions and get messages.

"The board president was put up there as a foil. He said what he was told to say. Even then he didn't know what he was saying."

"Finally, we had to settle for the good of the system," Vaughn said. "People said to me, 'You've got them by the jugular—stay out.' But we couldn't do that."

Byrd says the impasse developed because the board "simply didn't have the resources" to meet the teachers' demands.

"The board wanted to keep money for repairs and supplies," Byrd said. "No matter how popular it is to cry, 'Chop the top,' when you do that, you lose services. People are complaining now that our mail is slower than before at central office."

Such bickering between the board and union is seen by many labor analysts as part and parcel of their poor relations. Outsiders who have taken part in past negotiations and mediations have been taken aback at a bargaining relationship they find distinctly immature and counterproductive.

The students, board and union all suffered losses in the walkout.

"The board came out of the strike, as it always does, very badly," said Munoz. "And rightly so. When employees fight with the board and there is a disaster, it is fair play to say the board should have better relationships with its employees. One side has to be responsible."

Vaughn said: "We didn't come out looking like a rose. The current push for parental control of schools is a direct result of the lingering anger over our last struggle."

This is not the first time the cry for " Reform!" has gone out. In Springfield in the spring of 1985, calls for reform were in the air.

U.S. Education Secretary William Bennett was spearheading a nationwide campaign to improve education. In the Illinois legislature, there were dozens of "reform" proposals on the table.

Along with the proposals for more money, tougher courses and early childhood education, there was a bill that, at first blush, few lawmakers thought they could oppose.

Several teachers and a principal in Illinois had been arrested for child abuse in the past year. One had taught for more than a decade, moving from school to school, molesting children. He had an undetected criminal record.

At the same time, a private Chicago daycare center was the subject of an investigation of child molesting.

Bills were introduced to fingerprint child-care providers and teachers. The rationale was that repeat sex abusers could be identified and kept away from children.

Day-care operators expressed horror that any in their ranks would abuse a child, and, lacking strong representation, reluctantly agreed to let their workers be fingerprinted.

The teachers also expressed outrage at child abuse, but said "no" to fingerprints. They said it would make them look like criminals. They cited statistics that parents were more likely to abuse their children than were teachers. They maintained that they were, after all, a cut above child-care workers.

It was a loud, resounding, pull-out-all-the-stops "no," an example of the power of the teacher unions to kill legislation they do not like.

Union leaders passed out buttons with a red slash across a thumbprint. They called on their friends in labor to round up votes. Lawmakers were reminded of the contributions in money and workers their campaigns had received. The Illinois Education Association and the Illinois Federation of Teachers, normally archrivals, worked together for a change to fight the hated fingerprint bill.

In the end, a watered-down version of the law was passed, requiring criminal background checks of new teachers.

Current teachers—most of them dues-paying union members—were exempt.

The unions had won.

Photo by Paul F. Gero

Changing of the guard: Robert Healey congratulates Vaughn after she was approved by CTU members to succeed Healey as head of the union.

Saddled with responsibility, principals have little authority

Principal Edwin Tyska walked out of Von Humboldt Elementary School one day last year to discover that $600 of damage had been done to his car, parked just outside of the school. Gang insignias were carved into the paint. The trunk was bashed in. The tires were slashed.

So this year, he parked his car in a secret spot some blocks away and walked to his school at 2620 W. Hirsch St.

Being a principal in the Chicago Public Schools is a job that often bears little resemblance to the role that most people might imagine.

To be effective leaders, principals say, they must work around the system, selectively follow and ignore orders, and look the other way when unrealistic school board policies are violated.

Principals have become so frustrated with their status, they say, that they are seeking collective bargaining rights covering salary and working conditions. New York City principals have such rights.

Principals have to worry about security, supplies, home lives of the students, union grievances, conflicting instructions from the central office, excessive paperwork and the near-impossibility of firing anyone who does not do an acceptable job.

At Crane High, Principal Donald Collins says his top worry is the school's nearly 50 doors.

None can be locked from the inside because of the fire code. So Collins hopes his security force is alert enough to see that the doors don't open to let outsiders sneak in from the violent, gang-ridden neighborhood around the school at 2245 W. Jackson Blvd.

Although principals have the ultimate responsibility for what happens in their schools, they say they do not always have the authority to do the job well.

Warren Franczyk, principal of Bethune Elementary at 3030 W. Arthington St., did not even know who his new 8th-grade teacher would be for the second semester until three school days before she walked in. He had been using substitutes all first semester after his regular teacher took a sick leave.

"I had been interviewing candidates for months, trying to find just the right person," he said. "Finally I called personnel and asked how much time I had. They said, 'You're too late. We're sending someone out Monday.'"

In many cases, principals have to resort to somewhat devious means.

For example, assistant principals in elementary schools often have to teach part of the time because the system does not provide enough staff. At Goudy Elementary, 5120 N. Winthrop Ave., Principal Thomas J. McDonald admits that he "creatively" uses federal money to fund a position so he can free his assistant principal to help him run the school.

At Bethune, Franczyk structures the school day so his teachers get a lunch break free from the job of watching children, something they are not supposed to have under the union contract in a closed campus where children stay for lunch and have no recess.

"Teachers on one-half of each floor eat while other teachers or office workers keep an eye on the students," Francyzk said. "Teachers need this kind of a break to be effective. But don't tell the central office. We would all get in trouble."

Union contracts covering teachers and other employees have stripped principals of much authority.

Principals are the only nonunion employees in the schools. They are not in charge of lunchroom or custodial staffs, so they don't have the official clout to tell the building engineer to fix or clean anything. Officially, they are not even supposed to have keys to their schools. Unofficially, they do.

"You work out good relationships," Franczyk said, "or you don't get anything done."

Nevertheless, the job is coveted as the major route to higher posts and increased pay.

The average age of a principal in Chicago Public Schools is 51. The average salary is $53,871, based on the enrollment of the school as well as a principal's tenure.

This March, more than 1,700 candidates took the written principals' exam, the first time one has been given in five years. In 1983, only 168 out of 1,575 people who took the test passed both the written and oral sections.

The Chicago Principals Association, a union affiliated with the American Federation of School Administrators, AFL-CIO, is appealing a ruling by the Illinois Educational Labor Relations Board denying their request to collectively bargain a contract with the Chicago Board of Education.

Bargaining rights are crucial because of the inequities that principals face, said Loretta Nolan, former president of the association. "We have principals who have to take lunchroom duty and playground duty because the teachers refuse and are protected by their contract."

Nolan said principals are worn down by unrealistic expectations: "When money is cut, when staff is taken from your budget, they say, 'Be creative.' Well, you can work harder and smarter, but there is a limit.

"It is a dreamland fantasy that drives you up the wall."

Vaughn hears other side, then strikes like a shark

Jacqueline Vaughn is ready to roll up the sleeves of her flashy designer suits when it's time for the leader of what may be the most powerful teachers union local in the country to bargain for her members.

"I am no shrinking violet when I'm negotiating for my members' rights as professionals," said Vaughn, president of the Chicago Teachers Union, during a rare private interview at a downtown coffee shop before the union election where she won another term.

"I'll listen to what you have to say, but in the end I will do what I think needs to be done."

Vaughn, CTU president since 1984, was confident that she would be re-elected.

"If people don't know what I stand for and what I have done they have been asleep for the past four years," said Vaughn. "I think my record speaks for itself."

Vaughn's strategy for negotiating with the Chicago Board of Education is simple but firm: "Money talks or teachers walk."

Though union leaders have traditionally demanded other contract improvements such as class size reductions or increased medical benefits, a raise is the only thing that has pulled teachers off the picket lines.

That single-minded bargaining style has sent teachers out on nine strikes in 19 years, including two under Vaughn's leadership.

Those walkouts have produced contract provisions that labor lawyers say has greatly diluted the power of the school administration.

When Vaughn makes weekly school visits to keep in touch with her members, she often delivers impassioned speeches that keep the us-against-them spirit alive in the lull between negotiations.

"We are tired of being given mandates, dictates, instructions and directives from everybody when we are not asked to give our input," Vaughn told a group of teachers at Philip H. Sheridan Elementary, 9000 S. Exchange Ave.

"We don't tell them what to do in their kitchens so why should they tell us what to do in our classrooms," said Vaughn, eliciting a round a frenzied applause from the school staff.

During a post-strike union meeting last year, Vaughn called the board's plan to fund a raise with teacher layoffs, "the last gasps of a dying bird," referring to School Supt. Manford Byrd Jr. She also suggested that "the big bird flap his wings and head south for the winter."

Vaughn's obvious dislike for her bargaining foe hasn't mellowed since that meeting. Vaughn regularly referred to the superintendent as "Byrdbrain" during the coffeshop interview.

Vaughn, who was born 53 years ago in St. Louis, gave up her original dream of being a nurse and started on the path that led to the CTU presidency because a woman she calls "Aunt Mae" assured her that she would never have to worry about job security if she became a teacher.

After her parents died, she moved to Chicago's South Side to live with Alice Mae Bibbs, who for 35 years taught 1st grade at Stephen A. Douglas Elementary, now Douglas Community Academy. Aunt Mae died in September, 1986.

Vaughn graduated from Morgan Park High and Chicago Teachers College with a master's degree in special education. Before becoming active in union affairs, she taught at Boosfield Elementary, 1415 E. 70th St., and Einstein Elementary, 3830 S. Cottage Grove Ave., where she headed the special education department. She also worked in an administrative post as a language arts consultant at the district level.

When asked about her flashy approach to clothing, Vaughn said: "It's simple. I'm a shopaholic. For me, shopping is like therapy. It helps me deal with stress. When other people are going to lunch, I'm going shopping.

"During the last stike I would run out, even if it was just for a minute, to buy a scarf or a pair of hose and it made me feel better afterward."

Vaughn was named one of the city's 10 best-dressed black women in a survey last fall. Her flamboyant style is so closely associated with her image that some reporters took note of what she wore each day of the four-week strike to see if she ever wore the same thing twice.

She didn't.

Vaughn was elected CTU vice president in 1972, the same year that Robert Healey was elected to his first of four terms as president, and spent the next years in the shadows of white male union bosses.

In 1983, a personal conflict between Healey and then Supt. Ruth Love, a black woman, hurt the union's image in the black community. To negate the racial issue, Vaughn said, she was named to be the CTU official who made the televised union pronouncements about negotiations.

"When they first put me out there, I thought I was going to be the sacrifical lamb," she said.

If so, the lamb survived and union delegates voted Vaughn president the next year, after Healey resigned to become secretary-treasurer and later president of the Chicago Federation of Labor.

She earns $63,000 a year in union salary, and also serves as vice president of the Illinois Federation of Teachers, the American Federation of Teachers and Illinois State Federation of Labor.

She also sits on the board of directors of the Regional Transportation Authority, the Michael Reese Health Plan, the Big Brothers and Big Sisters of Greater Chicago and Amalgamated Trust and Savings Bank, positions that push her annual salary close to $100,000.

Vaughn is neither modest at the bargaining table, nor when talking about her accomplishments.

"No other leader in this union had to go through what I went through. I negotiated the first multi-year contract. I was the first one to negotiate benefits. I am trying to see what we can do to put a lasting impact on the community so they feel good about public schools."

But Vaughn sent her own son, Karl, now 27, to the private University of Chicago Laboratory school from kindergarten through his freshman year of high school when he transferred to Whitney Young Magnet High School.

Before the beginning of his sophomore year, Vaughn said, Karl declared that he wanted to go to a public school, "and I said fine. The lab school was too expensive anyway."

Vaughn's first husband, Theodore H. Wright, who is Karl's father, handles community relations in the board's high school field office. She presently is married to Robert Vaughn, a childhood friend, who is vice president of the meat cutters union.

Comparing her public posture and her private life, Vaughn said: "I get very little time to be the private me.

"I am a warm and compassionate person, really I am. But warmth and compassion don't win raises, do they?"

Pep talk: *Teachers union President Jacqueline Vaughn keeps members up to date. "We are tired of being given mandates, dictates, instructions," she says.*

What's wrong with this picture? *It's midday and a
7th grade teacher at Bethune Elementary has walked
out. "It happen a lot," says one student. Classrooms
without teachers are a chronic problem in the
Chicago Public Schools.*

Bureaucrats bungle
as young opportunities are lost

'I think I had more subs
than regular teachers'

Jaton Felton arrives at Du Sable High School to find that her typing class has no teacher, not even a substitute to keep order. It is not the first time, nor is this an isolated case.

On an average day in Chicago Public Schools, more than 5,700 students, like 15-year-old Jaton, have no teacher. Sometimes an adult shows up to watch over them, sometimes not.

It is as if all the grade school students in Downers Grove and Oak Brook arrived at school to find that their teacher was absent and there was no substitute.

The inability to consistently provide teachers for students is the most striking failure of an administration that fails to carry out even the most basic tasks of a school system.

But the Chicago school administration also does shockingly little to see that students come to school, that they are scheduled for a full day of instruction, that their classrooms have adequate supplies and that their school buildings are in good repair:

• At least 200 children in the Humboldt Park and West Town neighborhoods graduated from 8th grade and failed to show up for high school over the past three years. The school bureaucracy couldn't find them, but a social service agency did, and convinced them to give high school a try. Thousands of other dropouts slipped away, with no one trying to get them into class.

• Students at Phillips High piece together remnants of paperbacks to get enough intact books for class. An encyclopedia order for Phillips' library is lost for a year. Construction paper and paper clips must be rationed at Goudy Elementary. Buckets are used to catch water in the top-floor library of Howe Elementary.

• Calvin Reavers, 15, plays cards during a study hall at Bowen High, one of three 40-minute study halls scheduled for his 6-hour day. Thousands of high school students are cheated of entire courses each year because their schedules are heavily padded with study halls.

Teaching Chicago's schoolchildren is not an easy job. Money is perennially tight, the employee unions are demanding, many students from poor and broken families are behind even before they enter kindergarten.

But society—through its government—has given the Chicago Board of Education and its administrators this task. It is their job. They are not doing it.

Chicago School Supt. Manford Byrd Jr. says he would like to allow students to take more courses and fewer study halls, but "that would be buying more teacher time."

Byrd says he is surprised by the number of teacherless classes. He says parents are to blame for not getting children to school. When asked about leaking roofs and lacking supplies, Byrd says money is hard to come by. But he says it from a plush office while being paid a $100,000 salary, surrounded by thousands of bureaucrats.

Chicago Board of Education headquarters, called "Pershing Gardens" by school critics, is in a former warehouse at 1819 W. Pershing Rd. that has been renovated over the past five years at a cost of $22 million.

The nearly 3,000 people who work at the offices on the South Side listen to piped-in music, walk on thick carpets and enjoy a panoramic view of the city from their 5th-floor cafeteria.

They live in a world apart from the principals, teachers and children who spend their days in schools that are often dirty, unpainted and ill-equipped, buildings that may resemble fortresses more than centers of learning.

The isolation of school policymakers from the 419,537 children they are supposed to serve is a prime cause of the institutionalized child neglect taking place in the public schools.

The bureaucratic structure of the public schools is so inbred and permeated with political networks that former school board President George Munoz says: "People step into the shoes that have always been there. They fill the shoes. They die or move on, but the shoes remain."

A seven-month examination of the schools by The Tribune, which included interviews with hundreds of students, parents, teachers, principals and administrators, found a school system run by career bureaucrats whose priorities are out of touch with those who work in the schools and insensitive to the needs of children.

Du Sable teacher Herbert Tarnor uses a scavenged popcorn popper to heat chemistry experiments because he has no bunsen burners, but the school board builds a private bathroom for Clara Rosiles when she starts her administrative job as field superintendent.

Bethune Elementary goes an entire semester without a truant officer, but central office functionaries churn out curriculum guides that teachers find irrelevant. Manley High history teacher Burton Raimer calls a $10,000 high school curriculum guide "simplistic and full of cliches"; Bethune teacher Corla Hawkins says of a $29,000 grade school guide: "I figure I may be able to use it if I ever teach middle-class kids on the North Side."

The supply budget of Carter Elementary, 5740 S. Michigan Ave., is slashed to $578.71 from $3,000 to help pay for teacher raises, but the board pays $200 a month to a suburban Riverwoods company to water, trim and move plants around at the central office.

The public schools are headed by the Chicago Board of Education, a body of 11 members who are appointed to the unpaid posts by the mayor and confirmed by the City Council.

The board employs 42,389 people—more than any other entity in Illinois except the state government and Sears Roebuck and Co.

And although the board is officially vested with the authority to set policy, run the schools and control a $1.9 billion budget, the bureaucrats hold the purse strings and the power.

"The board approves 99 percent of all the recommendations of the administration," said Munoz.

No one can say for sure just how big the administration is. Although the board lists only 977 people on its administrative staff, 2,808 people work in the central office, and another 2,384 people work in district administrative offices, according to the board's most recent staff survey. Many of those people are not defined as administrators.

Some of those are top-level deputy or associate superintendents at salaries of $70,000 to $80,000 a year and are defined as certified teachers; others are typists at $13,000 to $18,000.

There are two chains of command within the administration. One is made up of the general superintendent (Byrd), one deputy superintendent (soon to be three) and 23 district superintendents. The 514 school principals report to the district superintendents.

Another chain of command goes from offices to departments to bureaus. The office of instructional services, for example, has five departments. Each department has from one to 11 bureaus. There are associate superintendents, assistant superintendents, directors, coordinators and facilitators.

In a school system in which two-thirds of the students come from poverty-stricken homes, the skewed priorities of the administration short-change children of some of the services they need most.

In one attempt to measure the true size of the administration, the Chicago Panel on Public School Policy and Fi-

nances, a citizens research group, counted one bureaucrat for every 123 children in the current year, an increase from one for every 158 students in 1981.

By contrast, the state average last year was one administrator for every 220 students, according to a State Board of Education report. In the same report, the Chicago system's bureaucrat-student ratio was put at 1 to 239.

At the same time, the Chicago system is short on people to help difficult students. The current budget shows one social worker for every 2,151 students, one truant officer for every 2,715 students and one psychologist for every 2,268 students.

The national rule of thumb for social workers, for example, is one for every 1,500 students—just to keep up with the paperwork. "For any kind of individual help, it would have to be even lower than 1,500," said Kim Knauer, a state board spokeswoman.

Byrd defends his administration and says that "invariably, when groups come in to look at us, they tell us we are understaffed for what we are trying to do.

"I want this administration to be as lean as it can be," Byrd said. "Is it sluggish? I don't know. A big system such as ours, I guess, is more like a battleship than a speedboat. You don't turn on the same arc."

Bell Elementary is a neighborhood school with a citywide magnet program for gifted children. It has impressively high reading and math scores, and last year finished first in the city for 8th-grade reading scores.

Principal Leo Priebe says parents and

teachers at the school, 3730 N. Oakley Ave., were disappointed when they heard nothing from the school board commending Bell students.

"Wouldn't it have been nice," Priebe said, "if we would have had a letter from somebody congratulating us for our achievement that I could have displayed on the school bulletin board?"

Donald Collins, principal of Crane High, 2245 W. Jackson Blvd., faces a different situation.

Crane is savaged by social problems. Ninety percent of the students live in public housing. The school has day care for children of its students and a birth control clinic, both funded in part by other government agencies. Reading and math scores are among the lowest in the city. The dropout rate is among the highest.

Asked if school officials have ever recognized Crane's special problems and given him resources to reach this difficult population, Collins thought for a moment. Then he shook his head.

"No," he said. "I can't think of one thing."

The lack of concern felt by Priebe and Collins is translated in more tangible ways to the system's 595 schools, filtering down to each child and falling the hardest on the most vulnerable.

• The roof at Howe Elementary, 720 N. Lorel Ave., has leaked for three years. Water drips through a warped ceiling tile into a bucket next to a slide projector in the library.

Children using the library in the all-black and predominately poor school to practice for an oratory contest are warned where to stand. Bernard Demb,

who teaches reading in the library, dries desks with paper towels.

Engineer Willard Drucker says he requested a new roof in April, 1985. He got an estimate of $23,664 in June, 1986. The work was approved Nov. 23, 1987. But the approval was meaningless, Drucker said, because he was told there was no money.

In March, Drucker asked that the leak in the 16-year-old roof be patched. He got the materials in April and the roof was patched May 13.

• In the basement of Howe, math specialist Loris Brown and a reading specialist teach in a storage room.

Pipes run across the ceiling. A noisy space heater cranks away. Children squeeze in between shelves of curriculum guides and copying paper. The reading specialist tries to grade papers over the noise of Brown's teaching.

"I'd love to have a room," Brown said, "but we have absolutely no space."

• The library at Manley High, 2935 W. Polk St., consists mostly of empty shelves. An entire paperback rack is bare.

The available books are not appropriate for high school students because the library has not been updated since Manley was a 7th- and 8th-grade school—15 years ago.

The lack of materials is especially acute because many Manley students belong to a street gang whose archrival controls the area around the closest public library branch, said English teacher Suzanne Lampka.

"This is settled gang territory, so that makes the school safer," said Lampka. "But it is bad because they can't go to the public library safely. We can't assign work that requires library research."

This year, Lampka used her own money to buy magazine subscriptions for students, brought bookshelves from home and searched used-book stores for encyclopedias, reference books and novels.

"These kids are survivors," Lampka said. "They are black young men still in school as seniors. They are the success of the neighborhood."

When the bureaucrats enter the picture, things change.

Principal Ernestine Curry of Phillips High, 244 E. Pershing Rd., received some needed supplies and repairs when the Board of Education scheduled its monthly meeting at her school.

In the two weeks before the board met there last school year, Curry got an office rug cleaned for the first time in 10 years. Stage lights that hadn't worked for 12 years were fixed, and dingy gray walls were painted.

"It's a joke among the principals," Curry said. "As soon as they hear where the board is going, they call and ask, 'What did you get?'"

Students barely noticed one Thursday when a 7th-grade teacher at Bethune, 3030 W. Arthington St., packed her purse, put on her coat and walked out in the middle of the day.

"It happen a lot," said one boy as the class waited for the school to find a spare adult to mind the class. "She probably have something to do."

Bethune Principal Warren Franczyk said the teacher has missed an average of one day a week this year and he is lowering her rating to "satisfactory" because of her absences.

Teacher absenteeism is epidemic in the Chicago schools. On an average day,

at least 1,070 teachers—4 percent of the staff—call in sick, and an average of 190 classes go unstaffed, according to school board records.

Actually, a larger number calls in sick, but some schools do not call the substitute center to request subs for all their absent teachers.

The absentee rate is higher on Mondays and Fridays, when an average of 1,117 teachers don't show up, and an average of 259 classes go unstaffed.

"We have unfilled orders almost every day; that's just a fact of life," Sharon Goldberg, director of the substitute teacher center, said in February. "It has always been like this. We are having a rough time now, and it will probably get worse as the year goes on."

It has.

The sub center could not fill the classes of all absent teachers on a single day from Jan. 22 through the middle of May.

During the first two weeks of May, the average number of unfilled classes was 405 a day—12,150 students with no teacher or, at best, an extra adult found to babysit. On Mondays and Fridays in early May, the average was 590 unfilled classes a day, or 17,700 students.

That would be equivalent to all the elementary students in Wilmette, Winnetka, Glencoe, Kenilworth, Glenview, Deerfield, Highland Park and Evanston arriving at school to find they had no teacher.

On average, Chicago teachers take 11 sick days during the 39 weeks they work each year, one more than the 10 they can take under their union contract without being docked. That is about double the average of teachers across the nation, who miss 5.7 days a year, and of U.S. workers overall, who are absent 7.2 days during a 12-month work year, according to the U.S. Bureau of Labor Statistics.

Although the school board employs 156 truant officers to check on students, no one monitors teachers' absences. "The resources of the school system do not allow for that," said Raymond Principe, director of teacher personnel.

The lack of teachers falls hardest on students who attend school in poor neighborhoods. Goldberg said many substitutes refuse assignments because "they want to work close to home or won't work in certain parts of the city."

In more affluent neighborhoods, principals have their own stock of substitutes—often teachers who live nearby—and don't rely solely on the sub center.

But in schools where children need the most, they often get the least.

Jaton Felton stomped out of her typing class one day this winter when there were 150 unfilled classes—due to the absences of 30 of Du Sable's 129 teachers—and demanded of a visitor: "Will you teach our class? We ain't got no teacher.

"No one shows up, no one tells us what is going on," said Jaton, a sophomore at the all-black school at 4934 S. Wabash Ave. whose students come primarily from public housing in the Robert Taylor Homes.

"They tell us we shouldn't be skipping our classes, and yet they have so many teachers skipping work that they can't find enough people to fill in for them."

Elementary schools, when short of substitutes, pull teacher aides, office workers or teachers who work with small groups of handicapped students off their regular duties to take care of classes.

Principals say they know that not all the teachers who call in sick are really sick.

"We see a pattern," said Bethune's Franczyk. "A teacher will take three days off a month, the same days every month. That's not sickness. That's personal."

In high school, substitutes are given lists of classrooms to cover, sometimes without any indication of the subjects to be taught.

Substitute teacher Rischelle Boykin had such a list one day in January at Du Sable, and she peered at it as she sat in front of a class of bored students.

"I don't even know what class this is," Boykin said. "It's just on my schedule to be here. We won't do anything. We'll just have a study hall."

Byrd expressed surprise when told there were classes without teachers in his schools.

"If that's happening, I would say that it is not a good situation," Byrd said.

Faced with parades of subs or teacherless classes, loaded up with study halls, forced to make do with skimpy supplies in shabby surroundings and largely deprived of what makes school interesting, many public school students make what seems to them to be the only logical decision—they leave.

Benita Burgess dropped out of Simeon Vocational High, 8235 S. Vincennes Ave., when she was a junior. Now 21, she lives in Englewood with her two preschool children.

"School wasn't very interesting," said

Burgess. "I think I had more subs than regular teachers. When a sub comes in, you find that it's kind of like a holiday."

Chicago's dropout problem grows out of its truancy problem. Neither is handled well by the school administration.

When students are absent from Chicago schools, no one looks too hard for them. Maybe a computer, programmed to call absent children, will phone home. Maybe a teacher will ask for a note if the child comes back. Then again, maybe not.

Glendalyn Lathom, 18, a senior at Westinghouse Vocational High, 3301 W. Franklin Blvd., wasn't worried about being caught playing hooky the day she and her sister, Joanne, skipped school.

"They don't know I'm absent," she said on one school day. "They take attendance, but if you miss, the kids say they saw you. They think you're there all day."

Westinghouse officials, called a few days later, said their records showed that Glendalyn had been in school that day. At Crane High, officials said they thought Joanne was in school.

Critics have charged that Chicago schools actually encourage cutting class to ease staff shortages and to get disruptive children out of school.

A 1986 study of six general high schools by the Chicago Panel on Public School Policy and Finance found that three-quarters of the surveyed students took six or fewer 40-minute courses each day. State law requires a minimum of 300 minutes of daily instruction. In Chicago, the difference is made up with study halls.

Even study halls can be mirages. The panel's research found that thousands of students were assigned on paper to nonexistent study halls at the beginning or the end of the day, encouraging students to skip out.

"Kids will cut class as long as school exists," said Jack Mitchell, field superintendent for high schools.

Chicago's official attendance rate is 91 percent for all schools, 85.2 percent for high schools. Outside Chicago, the average state attendance rate is 94.6 percent, close to the national goal of 95 percent.

Byrd blames parents for children's failure to attend school.

"It's just one more burden to lay on an urban school system," Byrd said. "The first line of defense in getting a kid to come to school is not the school. It is the home."

Parents surely hold primary responsibility. But in many communities, when parents fail, other parts of society—police, schools, social service agencies—form a safety net to catch children before they fall so far that they hurt themselves and the rest of society.

In Chicago, public school bureaucrats are failing to hold up their corner of the net.

Joseph Johnson had missed 21 days of 5th grade at Tilton Elementary, 233 N. Keeler Ave, before transferring schools. One day in March, he said he stayed home "to wait for our Social Security check."

Truant officer Almetta Gary did not know why Johnson was not at school, nor did she have a correct address for him. Joseph's chronic absenteeism is the type of behavior that educators say is the beginning step toward dropping out. Nearly 50 percent of Chicago students drop out of school, some

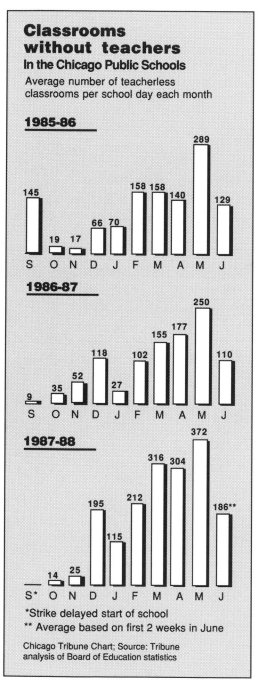

Classrooms without teachers
In the Chicago Public Schools
Average number of teacherless classrooms per school day each month

1985-86

1986-87

1987-88

*Strike delayed start of school
** Average based on first 2 weeks in June

Chicago Tribune Chart; Source: Tribune analysis of Board of Education statistics

before their freshman year.

For years, school officials contended that the system's dropout rate was only about 8 percent. What they didn't say was that that figure covered only a single year. A Chicago Panel study forced the school board to admit that the true high school dropout rate is close to 50 percent.

Rev. Charles Kyle, a Loyola University education professor who has studied high school dropouts in Chicago, got a contract from Illinois Atty. Gen. Neil Hartigan to research grade school dropouts.

Kyle says he needs the attorney general's help to force the school board to give him the necessary data. The board says it has no reliable statistics on how many children drop out of grade school.

Kyle believes that he will find that 10 percent of Chicago public grade school children drop out before high school, usually after 7th or 8th grade. That would push the city's dropout rate close to 60 percent.

"It's a considerable problem," said David Peterson, principal of Wells High, 936 N. Ashland Ave. "When they graduate from elementary school, many students feel they have all they need."

A Tribune survey of 16 high schools showed that they often do not know how many of the 8th graders they expect to enroll as freshmen actually show up.

Network for Youth Services, a coalition of Hispanic social service agencies, has completed tracking 136 out of 162 students who were supposed to be freshmen but never enrolled last fall at Clemente and Wells High Schools on the Near Northwest Side. Some had enrolled at other schools, some just disappeared. But 17 students who were located had dropped out; 10 of those were convinced to enter high school.

Over the past three years, the network has tracked nearly 1,000 such students.

"The network brought about 200 to 250 children into the schools in our attendance area—Districts 5 and 6 in West Town and Humboldt Park," said Joseph Ruiz, District 6 administrator. "We don't have the money or manpower to do that. They knocked on doors."

At Association House in Humboldt Park, Ivan Medina, director of youth and family services, estimates that 10 percent of the 12- and 13-year-olds in an after-school literacy program attend school only "once or twice every two weeks."

Steven Haymes, who helps run the program, thinks part of the fault lies with the contrast between the children's lives and what is taught in school.

"The schools talk about graduating and getting a job," Haymes said. "But the kids look around their neighborhood and that is not what they see. They do not see employed people, even if they have finished school.

"None of the problems these children face every day—drugs, gangs, alcoholic parents, poverty, living in transient hotels, seeing people shot in the street—is addressed in school," Haymes said. "The curriculum is boring. It is irrelevant. They drop out."

School board President Frank Gardner agrees that the schools must alter their curricula and methods if they are to reach the majority of Chicago school children.

"We have been trained to teach the middle-class child, the average child," Gardner said. "We have not learned the techniques and styles to teach youngsters who have experiences that do not lead to success in the schools."

Clara Rosiles is sitting in her administrator's office in Oscar Mayer Elementary, 2250 N. Clifton Ave. It is larger than the principal's office, larger than most classrooms. Rosiles picks up the phone when she wants to talk to a subordinate administrator in the next office, or her secretary in the office next to that.

Rosiles' office has a desk, a television, a sideboard, a bookshelf, four settees, a table with four chairs, six other chairs and a couch. There are paintings on the walls and sculpture on the shelves.

Across the hall, a separate bathroom was built for her.

Rosiles says she doesn't know how much it cost or where the money came from. The central office could not give details on the cost, either.

Rosiles is one of three field superintendents. The positions made up a new layer of bureaucracy when Byrd created them in 1985; he moved last month to abolish the jobs after persistent public criticism that they were unnecessary. At the same time, however, he increased the number of deputy superintendent jobs to three from one.

Rosiles does not know what she will do next.

Rosiles was asked to describe her duties:

"I have to remind the district superintendents of things. I remind them that they have to remind principals to follow board policies. I have to be sure board policies are followed."

Clara Rosiles is paid $65,723 a year.

Manford Byrd's view from the top

Chicago School Supt. Manford Byrd Jr. characterizes himself as "probably the most gifted urban administrator in this country."

He is a 34-year veteran of the school system. He's been a teacher, principal, administrative aide to the superintendent, deputy superintendent and chief operating officer. As superintendent, he makes $100,000 a year plus as much as $10,000 in bonuses.

But Byrd says he doesn't know what to do about the city's chronically ailing public school system.

"There's a problem," Byrd says, "of finding exactly what's needed to improve the schools—whether there are things you need to get in terms of materials, or if it's in terms of systems, or if it's in terms of a trained or different staff, or if it's in terms of a moderation of class size—a whole multiplicity of things."

Byrd says he doesn't know why Chicago public school children don't perform better on standardized tests.

"Either we're not working on the right things," he says, "or we're not using the right materials, or we haven't prepared them the right way, or the kids are not coming with the right preparation and they're not getting the support they need from the community."

And Byrd says he doesn't know why reading scores of the city's elementary school children rose during the late 1970s and early 1980s before leveling off five years ago.

"I cannot put my finger on what happened," Byrd says.

Attempting to answer these questions and others is "bedeviling," according to Byrd, and more research on educating urban children is needed.

"Doctors who deal with cancer are not afraid to say, 'I don't know what the cure is,'" he says.

Byrd, born May 29, 1928, in Brewton, Ala., started as a Chicago public elementary school teacher in 1954. Aided by black organizations lobbying for more representation in school leadership, he ascended the bureaucratic ladder to become the second highest official in the Chicago system and the top-ranking black in any major public school system in the nation by 1968.

Then he waited out a succession of superintendents.

His attempt to succeed Supt. James Redmond in 1975 was supported by black leaders, but the board selected Joseph Hannon, a white who had been an assistant superintendent.

Four years later, when Hannon resigned amid an escalating financial crisis, Byrd was passed over again—first for Angeline Caruso, a white associate superintendent who served on an inter-

Award Winner: *"I do an inordinate amount of speaking to groups. I give of my time, almost to a fault . . . I have been recognized by more community groups than all other superintendents together,"* Supt. Manford Byrd Jr. says.

im basis, and then for Ruth Love, a black who was school superintendent in Oakland, Calif.

"It's Byrd's turn," said the spokesman of a coalition of black ministers who took part in the unsuccessful effort on his behalf.

In fact, black leaders felt it was their turn. Byrd was their choice, and his continual rejection was a bitter reminder of the lack of black clout.

Three years later, things had changed.

Chicago had a black mayor elected by a black-dominated coalition.

So, when the school board voted on July 23, 1984, against renewing Love's contract, they didn't look far for her replacement.

He was sitting a few feet away in an anteroom. It was finally Byrd's turn.

Byrd's wife, Cheribelle, is head teacher at a public child-parent center on the South Side. Their three sons—Carl, Bradley and Donald—graduated from Lindblom Technical High.

Byrd rarely has a chance to go into the classrooms himself. He spends most of his work day at Board of Education offices at 1819 W. Pershing Rd., usually appearing around 8 a.m. and leaving around 6 p.m.

"Three or four times a week, there's something after 6:30 or 7, a dinner or reception or meeting of a parents group or business group," Byrd says.

"I do an inordinate amount of speaking to groups. I give of my time, almost to a fault."

Byrd is a courtly, soft-spoken, articulate man and is proud of the honors he receives. "I have been recognized," he says, "by more community groups than all other superintendents together."

Still, there are many, including some Byrd supporters, who contend that he is too sedentary, not aggressive enough in searching for solutions to the many problems of the schools.

Byrd doesn't like to hear criticism of the system or his stewardship. He describes such talk as "bashing" and blames it for the poor performance of students.

"Kids have an ambivalence," Byrd says. "They're told they should like school, but they read in the newspapers or see on TV that 'this is the pits.' "

The news media aren't the only villains, according to Byrd. He also blames past leaders of the system, a lack of money, the people who write the tests, the parents and the children.

"When you're all done," he says, "the learner must learn for himself or herself."

And Byrd blames those who cast blame. "Until the community, until the teachers, until the parents and until the administration stop scapegoating on each entity—until we do that—we're going to be working at counter-purposes," he says.

Byrd says he is often the object of unfair criticism.

He cites the school system's dismal scores on the American College Test (ACT), used by colleges in choosing applicants. Last year, half of Chicago's high schools ranked in the bottom 1 percent of all U.S. schools that gave the test.

Byrd notes that the students who took the test were seniors.

"Hell, I haven't had anything to do with any of them," he declares. "Those kids were in the pipeline for 12 years.

"Schools haven't gotten worse with me. We have made some data public that were not previously known. The making of this data public occurred during my watch. That doesn't mean I'm the cause of it."

Missing in Action: *Fifth-grader Joseph Johnson is*
not in school. His truant officer does not know why,
and does not have his correct address. Educators
say that chronic absenteeism is the first step toward
dropping out.

Chicago Board of Education

Of the 11 members of the Chicago Board of Education, four once were teachers, two are lawyers, two are education activists, one is a retired utility company executive, one is a banker and one is an official of a major community organization.

Ada Lopez, 41
Member since '87. Teacher for 12 years, former coordinator of bilingual education. University of Illinois-Chicago graduate. Northwest Sider's daughter attended public and private schools.

Frank Gardner, 64
President; member since '84. Teacher, principal and administrator in Chicago schools 35 years. South Side resident's three children attended parochial schools. De Paul, Northwestern graduate.

Michael Penn, 39
Member since '85. Lawyer, member of NAACP and Chicago Urban League. Graduate of Roosevelt University and De Paul Law School. West Sider sends his two school-age children to public schools.

William Farrow, 69
Vice president; member '84-88. Former executive of Commonwealth Edison who retired after 35 years. Roosevelt University graduate and South Side resident sent his two children to public schools.

Frances Davis, 54
Member since '86. Director of human services for Operation PUSH. South Side resident attended Roosevelt University. Her four children attended public schools in Evanston and Chicago.

Clark Burrus, 59
Member since '82. Senior vice president, First National Bank of Chicago, RTA board member and former city controller. Graduate of Roosevelt University. His one child attended public schools.

Mattie Hopkins, 68
Member since '85. Former public school teacher who retired after 32 years. Once served as union delegate. Graduate of Tuskegee Institute and the University of Chicago. South Sider has no children.

Winnie Slusser, 59
Member since '86. North Side activist and PTA leader 25 years. Member of three education study commissions. Graduate of Northwestern. Her five children graduated from Chicago public schools.

Patricia O'Hern, 56
Member, '77-80; reappointed, '85. Southwest Side PTA leader and activist for more than 20 years. Mercy High graduate's two children attended Chicago public schools.

Linda Coronado, 40
Member since '86. Former counselor at Tilden High is mayoral adviser on Latino affairs. Northeastern Illinois graduate. Southwest Side resident has two children in Chicago public schools.

George Munoz, 37
Member, '83-88; president '84-86. Partner in a Loop law firm and a CPA. Brownsville, Tex., native holds degrees from University of Texas, De Paul and Harvard. Bachelor lives on South Side.

Comparing property tax revenues

1986 taxes, Chicago and suburbs

Equalized assessed valuation per pupil	Property tax rate for local schools*	Property tax revenue per pupil
Dollar averages	Per $100 assessed valuation	Dollar averages
Chicago	**Chicago**	**Chicago**
$38,390	$3.776	$1,447
Suburban average	**Suburban average**	**Suburban average**
69,483	4.617	3,208
Suburban Cook County	**Suburban Cook County**	**Suburban Cook County**
73,498	4.734	3,479
Du Page County	**Du Page County**	**Du Page County**
70,911	4.419	3,133
Lake County	**Lake County**	**Lake County**
61,404	4.435	2,724

*Suburban tax rates are averages based on all local education taxes;
for Chicago, it is a total of all such rates except the School Finance Authority

Source: Chicago Tribune analysis of data from Illinois State
Board of Education, Chicago Board of Education; county clerks of Cook, Lake and
Du Page Counties

Chicago school revenues per pupil
By source; adjusted for inflation

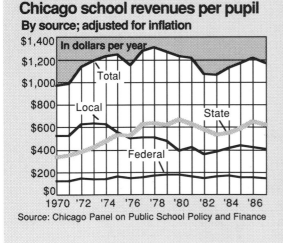

Source: Chicago Panel on Public School Policy and Finance

Chicago Tribune Graphic; Source: School districts

Per pupil property tax
Comparing property tax revenues in major public school districts
In dollars per pupil for the 1986-87 school year

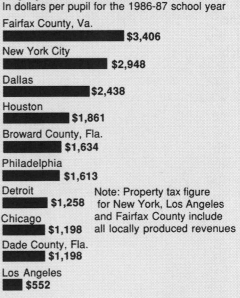

Fairfax County, Va. $3,406
New York City $2,948
Dallas $2,438
Houston $1,861
Broward County, Fla. $1,634
Philadelphia $1,613
Detroit $1,258
Chicago $1,198
Dade County, Fla. $1,198
Los Angeles $552

Note: Property tax figure for New York, Los Angeles and Fairfax County include all locally produced revenues

City brings up rear in providing taxes for education

No other district has so many hard-to-teach children

Chicago provides less property tax money per pupil for its public schools than any other community in Cook or Du Page Counties, a Tribune analysis of tax and school records has found.

Even when funds from the state and federal governments are added in, the city's school system has to operate on about 15 percent less money per student than schools in the average suburb, the study determined.

But a Tribune Poll found that Chicagoans are so concerned about how bad the schools are that a majority say they would be willing to pay more in taxes to make them better. A separate Tribune survey of 68 top executives of a broad range of major employers in the city and its suburbs also found substantial support for higher school taxes.

The findings of the study and the poll and survey, undertaken as part of The Tribune's seven-month examination of the schools, rebut the repeated assertions of politicians.

For years, powerful city and state politicians have opposed increased funding for the city's schools, contending that voters would not approve a tax increase and that the school system did not need more money.

But the city's schools, which have far and away the most difficult job of any school district in Illinois, are chronically money-starved. Caught in the cross fire of political skirmishing, Chicago schools are routinely short-changed both in City Hall and in the Illinois General Assembly:

• In Chicago, political leaders, who exercise indirect control over the school system, keep the property-tax rate for the schools lower than those of nearly every community in the metropolitan area. They do this to permit other taxing bodies, such as the city government, to raise more from property owners without risking a voter backlash.

But the combination of that low school tax rate and Chicago's low property wealth means that city schools receive only $1,447 per student per year in property tax revenue. That's less than half of the $3,208 per student that an average suburban district gets in property-tax money.

And in many sections of the suburbs, the gap is even wider. For example, the Tribune study found that the combination of high school and elementary school tax levies imposed last year within Niles High School District 219 brought in an average of $5,555 per student, or nearly three times more than the $1,447 raised in Chicago.

• In Springfield, state legislators—enmeshed in regional conflicts among the city, suburbs and Downstate—manipulate the state school aid "equalization" formula to benefit affluent suburban districts at the expense of Chicago and other poor communities. They do this even though the stated purpose of the formula is to help tax-poor districts and schools with hard-to-teach children from low-income families.

In refusing to provide more money, city and state politicians argue that the school system is a financial sinkhole, that it wastes money now and would waste more if it had more.

"How is more money going to solve it?" asks State Senate Minority Leader James "Pate" Philip, chairman of the Du Page County Republican Party.

"We've given them more money and more money and more money, and the system seems to get worse. What they're doing is not working and has never worked. Why should we fuel the system? It's a bottomless pit."

Yet, the problems of Chicago schools cannot be blamed entirely on bad leadership.

No other district in the state has as many hard-to-teach children. Chicago's 595 public elementary and high schools have only about a quarter of the state's total public school enrollment, but more than half of all low-income students in Illinois. In addition, nearly four of every five Illinois students with limited proficiency in English are in Chicago Public Schools.

Such children need more individual attention, but city schools don't have the money to provide it.

This lack of money has been a major component in the failure of the school system to educate its students, and, over the decades, this failure has short-changed millions of children.

Continued failure will mean not only a bleak life for more generations of children, but also a growing social price to the entire state in welfare costs, crime, lost taxes and a threat to the metropolitan economy because of a projected shortage of young people educated well enough to get jobs in the modern workplace.

Chicago's public schools live in poverty.

In the 1985-86 school year, the system had total revenues from state, local and federal sources of $3,957 per enrolled student—nearly $800 less per pupil than the average suburban community.

Financial support is also low when compared with other large districts across the country.

Among the 10 largest school districts in the nation, Chicago ranked 7th in total revenues per pupil for the 1986-87 school year. In that year, Chicago raised $3,928 per pupil, nearly $2,000 less than New York City.

Chicago was also behind Fairfax County, Va., a suburb of Washington, D.C. ($5,633); Philadelphia ($5,236); Detroit ($4,126); Dade County, Fla., which includes Miami ($3,964); and Broward County, Fla. which includes Ft. Lauderdale ($3,940). It ranked ahead of Los Angeles ($3,642); Dallas ($3,623); and Houston ($3,178).

A major reason for Chicago's low financial ranking is the heavy reliance in Illinois on the use of property tax revenues to finance education.

This means that a district with a wealthy population, or with lots of valuable industrial or commercial property, has a relatively easy time raising money for its schools while a district serving a poor community, such as Chicago, must struggle to get by.

The state school aid formula is supposed to even out such inequities by giving more money to tax-poor districts and more money to districts with children from poor families, according to Michael A. Belletire, associate superintendent for finance and support services for the State Board of Education.

"Chicago has had to bear a burden that no other school district has had to bear," Belletire said of the city's poverty population.

"The state's role is to recognize the fact that it's a lot easier to educate kids from similar backgrounds with a relatively high socio-economic background. Therein lies the justification for the state to step in and act as broker."

But, because of the politics of the state and the state legislature, the aid formula falls far short of its stated goal.

According to one measure (federal census data), 45 percent of the 419,537 students enrolled in Chicago schools are from low-income families. According to another (the number of children eligible for the federal school meal program), the figure is 68.1 percent.

But the state aid formula pretends that only 22.6 percent of the city students are from poor families. In fact, it pretends that no school district in the state has a low-income enrollment that is more than 22.6 percent of the total student population.

This artificial limit ends up costing Chicago schools as much as $121 million a year—about $280 per pupil—in state aid that they would receive if the formula were to function freely, according to a Tribune analysis.

That $280 per student would reduce the funding gap between the city and suburban schools by about a third, but the city schools would still have about $520 less per pupil than the average suburban district.

The distortion of the state aid formula is done by the General Assembly and the governor so that Chicago schools get slightly less than a third of the total state budget for elementary and secondary education—the arbitrary limit that has been in effect for years.

"They beat on the formula until it comes out the way they want it," says David Chicoine, a professor at the University of Illinois, Urbana, and an adviser to Downstate legislators on the school aid formula.

This school year, Chicago schools will get $718.8 million from the state, or slightly more than a third of the system's $1.8 billion budget.

That money, the bulk of which is allocated under the aid formula, represents 30.8 percent of all state funds for elementary and secondary education.

Many legislators contend that 30.8 percent is a very generous figure because the Chicago school system has only 23.6 percent of the state's public school students.

They tend to overlook the fact that Chicago has 54.2 percent of the state's public school children from low-income families.

Public schools and property taxes

Chicago area unit school district equivalents

Tribune analysis of 1986* property tax revenues

The Chicago public schools constitute a unit district, including elementary schools and high schools. For this study, every suburban high school district that isn't a unit district was grouped with the elementary districts or portions of elementary districts that feed students into it. In this way, unit districts were created on paper that could be compared with Chicago.

Districts (Combined with local feeder school districts)	Property tax revenue per pupil (rank)	Equalized assessed valuation per pupil (rank)	Average combined tax rate (rank)	Districts (Combined with local feeder school districts)	Property tax revenue per pupil (rank)	Equalized assessed valuation per pupil (rank)	Average combined tax rate (rank)
Niles Twp. 219	$5,555 (1)	$142,804 (2)	$3,890 (49)	Lake Park 108	2,912(31)	62,374(32)	4.683(20)
Lake Forest 115	5,236(2)	157,508(1)	3.322(55)	Lake Zurich U. 95	2,857(32)	68,217(27)	4.188(25)
Glenbrook 225	5,182(3)	116,852(5)	4.435(31)	Downers Gr. 99	2,839(33)	68,481(26)	4.146(39)
New Trier 203	5,055(4)	96,961(9)	5.213(11)	Warren 121	2,806(34)	61,616(33)	4.554(40)
Maine Twp. 207	5,025(5)	75,099(21)	NA	Libertyville 128	2,757(35)	70,127(24)	3.933(28)
Hinsdale Twp. 86	4,859(6)	116,823(6)	3.990(44)	Naperville U. 208	2,732(36)	63,742(29)	4.286(36)
Evans. Twp. 202	4,661(7)	71,042(23)	6.709(3)	Proviso Twp. 209	2,715(37)	59,273(37)	4.580(27)
Deerfld.-H.P. 113	4,618(8)	92,803(12)	4.976(17)	Zion-Benton 126	2,660(38)	50,595(44)	5.258(9)
Lyons Twp. 204	4,596(9)	96,214(10)	4.767(23)	Wheaton U. 200	2,632(39)	63,417(30)	3.925(48)
Ridgewood 234	4,552(10)	130,806(4)	3.480(53)	Oak Lawn 218	2,632(40)	59,513(36)	4.422(32)
Stevenson 125	4,441(11)	94,386(11)	4.705(24)	Homewood 233	2,621(41)	51,228(42)	5.117(16)
N.W. Twp. 214	4,363(12)	97,848(8)	4.459(29)	West Chicago 94	2,618(42)	50,883(43)	5.144(15)
Westmont U. 201	4,003(13)	76,049(20)	5.263(8)	Rich Twp. 227	2,574(43)	37,973(51)	6.778(2)
Fenton 100	3,955(14)	98,659(7)	4.008(43)	Indian Pr. U. 204	2,477(44)	62,738(31)	3.947(45)
Barrington U. 220	3,846(15)	91,572(13)	4.200(38)	Bloom Twp. 206	2,366(45)	32,881(54)	7.195(1)
Oak Pk.-R.F. 200	3,843(16)	58,368(38)	6.584(4)	Thornton Fr. 215	2,361(46)	40,689(49)	4.790(21)
Evergrn. Pk. 231	3,839(17)	78,160(18)	4.912(18)	Morton 201	2,222(47)	54,821(41)	4.054(42)
Elmhurst U. 205	3,674(18)	85,309(16)	4.306(34)	Thornton 205	2,118(48)	40,689(49)	5.206.(13)
Lisle Unit 202	3,595(19)	85,051(17)	4.226(37)	Grayslake 127	2,078(49)	36,731(52)	5.656(5)
Leyden 212	3,553(20)	132,886(3)	2.674(56)	Grant 124	2,036(50)	50,141(45)	4.061(41)
Pal.-Schaum. 211	3,512(21)	67,346(28)	5.215(10)	Antioch 117	1,884(51)	42,276(48)	4.457(30)
Riverside-Br. 208	3,392(22)	86,231(15)	3.934(46)	Wauconda U. 118	1,721(52)	46,795(47)	3.678(52)
Reavis 220	3,352(23)	87,292(14)	3.840(50)	Bremen 228	1,718(53)	28,499(55)	5.467(6)
Du Page 88	3,341(24)	77,386(19)	4.298(35)	Waukegan U. 60	1,536(54)	32,954(53)	4.662(26)
Elm. Pk. U. 401	3,333(25)	69,228(25)	4.777(22)	Chicago U. 299	1,447(55)	38,390(50)	3.776(51)
Oak Lawn 229	3,243(26)	74,084(22)	4.377(33)	N. Chicago 123	804(56)	16,423(57)	4.896(19)
Palos 230	3,099(27)	59,989(35)	5.166(47)	Round Lake 116	556(57)	16,429(56)	3.387(54)
Glenbard Twp. 87	2,977(28)	56,067(40)	5.309(14)	**Averages**			
Argo 217	2,952(29)	56,699(39)	5.206(7)	Cook suburbs	3,479	73,498	4.734
Mundelein 120	2,927(30)	60,786(34)	4.821(12)	Du Page County	3,133	70,911	4.419
				Lake County	2,724	61,404	4.435
				Suburban totals	3,208	69,483	4.617

*Collected in 1987   NA = Not available

Combined tax rates are per $100 of equalized assessed valuation

Chicago Tribune Graphic

"If you're interested in providing equity of schooling, then you want the kids with the most needs getting more dollars," says G. Alfred Hess, executive director of the Chicago Panel on Public School Policy and Finance, a citizens group that studies city school issues. "Chicago should get more money."

It's not just the artificial limit on low-income students that strips money from Chicago and other poor districts. There's also the flat grant.

No matter how rich a school district is, the formula gives it a flat grant per pupil. This year, the guaranteed flat grant is $144.

Thus, a wealthy district, such as Lake Forest High School District 115, which raised more than $7,000 per pupil in property taxes last year, can still receive about $200,000 in state aid under the flat grant provision.

What this means is that rich districts get thousands in state money for which they have little need, and that leaves less state money available for poor districts, desperate for financial help.

"It's basically a political decision," says Hess. "The theory was that everybody should get something so they'd be for higher taxes.

"The theory's false. Those suburban district representatives are the worst of the no-more-money-for-the-schools people. Giving them a flat grant hasn't helped."

Chicago schools are poor because the city itself is poor. Despite the economic strength of the downtown area, Chicago has much less property wealth than the suburbs, as measured by equalized assessed valuation. This is the value of

property as it is assessed for tax purposes and modified so that assessment levels throughout Illinois are relatively equal.

Taken together, the suburbs of Cook, Du Page and Lake Counties have an equalized assessed value of property of $69,483 per public school student.

In Chicago, the figure is $38,390.

This means that, overall, suburban tax rates have to be only about half as large as Chicago's to raise the same amount of money.

In addition, the Chicago schools have a lot more competition for property tax dollars than do those in the suburbs.

The total property tax rate in Chicago is just over $10.35 per $100 assessed value, one of the highest in Cook County, but only about 36 percent of that goes to schools. (If one includes the tax rate for the School Finance Authority, set up to issue bonds to pay off debts that resulted in the Chicago school system's financial collapse in 1979, the school figure rises to 40 percent.)

In the suburbs, school tax rates make up an average of about 60 percent of the total property tax rate.

"We pay a fantastic amount for police and fire protection in Chicago," says Hess. "People in the city expect to have health clinics where they can send indigent people.

"This city is in the cruel box of having to decide which services to provide to poor families. The schools are the service that's currently being short-changed. We're providing so many basic-need services to enable these people to live that we're not giving them the services requisite to escape the situation."

School Supt. Manford Byrd Jr. says: "It doesn't take a genius to know we're all operating off the same tax base. It's a matter of who gets there first."

Nonetheless, the financial and educational problems of the city's schools have gotten so bad that a small number of officials, such as State School Supt. Ted Sanders, are suggesting a Chicago property tax increase.

There is, however, a practical limit.

If the city increased school tax rates by 22 percent, so that they equaled the average suburban tax rate, an additional $138 million a year would be raised, or $325 more per student.

That would still leave a large gap between the city and suburban schools.

For Chicago to equal the suburban average of $3,208 in property tax revenues per pupil, city school tax rates would have to more than double, to $8.36 per $100 assessed value. That would increase the city's total tax rate to more than $14.93, higher than anywhere in Cook County except a section of south suburban Chicago Heights.

Many people outside of Chicago recognize the need to improve the city schools. "For the state, there is absolutely nothing as important as public education," says State Rep. Mary Lou Cowlishaw (R., Naperville), a member of the House Primary and Secondary Education Committee. "I don't think there is anyone—at least, any reasonable person—who would not give almost anything to decisively improve the Chicago schools."

The Tribune poll, conducted in mid-February, found that two of every three suburbanites believe that the well-being of Chicago has an effect on the suburbs, but there was a catch.

By a 9-to-1 ratio, suburban residents oppose any effort to get them to pay more for city schools, and only a third of the suburbanites think a lack of funds is a major city school problem.

Suburban legislators echo those sentiments. "The city of Chicago chose to have that system," says Rep. Jane Barnes (R., Palos Heights).

State Sen. Philip agrees, and he has gone so far this year as to propose legislation, dubbed "a reverse Robin Hood bill" by opponents, that would take money away from school districts with low achievement-test scores, such as Chicago, and give it to districts with high marks, such as those in Philip's home Du Page County. The bill could eventually cost Chicago schools $45 million a year in state aid.

But not all legislators are in the Philip camp.

State Sen. John Maitland (R., Bloomington) says: "This is one Downstater who is not going to try to take money away from Chicago. Chicago needs more money."

He notes that his stand is somewhat unusual. "People Downstate say, 'Enough is enough. We can only do so much.' Some Downstaters believe we should just take money from Chicago, East St. Louis, Danville, and pass it around," Maitland says. "There are going to be some who are going to be anti-Chicago no matter what we do."

But those legislators from outside of Chicago who recognize the need to help the city schools are hamstrung, Maitland says, by the failure of Chicago leaders, particularly school officials and

House Speaker Michael Madigan (D., Chicago), to make a strong push for more money.

Last spring, Madigan, who represents a mostly white district on the Southwest Side and whose children attend private schools, blocked Gov. James Thompson's attempt to increase the state income tax to raise more money for schools.

"Downstate legislators who would have been willing to support a tax increase weren't willing to be out in front," Maitland says. "Why should they stick their necks out if Madigan wasn't going to support it?"

Steve Brown, a spokesman for Madigan, contends that Madigan wasn't responsible for the failure of the tax increase, but he adds, "Madigan remained unconvinced of the need for a tax increase because there were other available revenues that could have been used for education."

Supt. Byrd says the needs of the public schools simply got lost amid conflicting political agendas.

"It had to do with politics beyond the school system," Byrd says. "The school system was just one ploy in the whole thing. The reason it didn't happen down there had to do with some politics beyond the politics of the board of education. We were the victims."

But the real victims are the children.

"I bet most of (the state legislators) picture our schools as places where gun-crazy gang-bangers chase around pregnant teenagers and spray graffiti all over the place," says Zakiyyah S. Muhammad, a security worker at the Coleman Elementary School on the South Side.

"We have a lot of problems. We are not trying to say that we don't. But that doesn't mean that they should turn their back on us.

"It doesn't mean that our children don't deserve an education."

Intervention: *Counselor Barbara Boxton tries to help a student, but there is only so much a school counselor can do.*

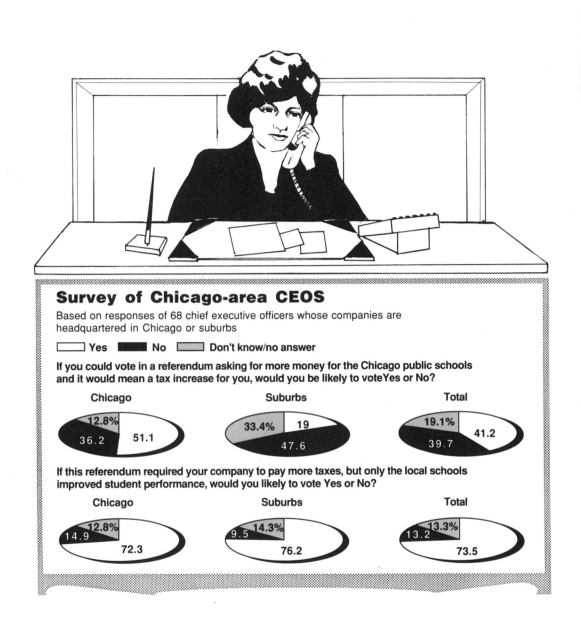

Survey of Chicago-area CEOS

Based on responses of 68 chief executive officers whose companies are headquartered in Chicago or suburbs

☐ Yes ■ No ▨ Don't know/no answer

If you could vote in a referendum asking for more money for the Chicago public schools and it would mean a tax increase for you, would you be likely to vote Yes or No?

Chicago	Suburbs	Total
12.8% / 36.2 / 51.1	33.4% / 19 / 47.6	19.1% / 39.7 / 41.2

If this referendum required your company to pay more taxes, but only the local schools improved student performance, would you likely to vote Yes or No?

Chicago	Suburbs	Total
12.8% / 14.9 / 72.3	14.3% / 9.5 / 76.2	13.3% / 13.2 / 73.5

City's willing to pay
for improved schools, poll finds

'Is there anything better
to spend money on?'

Chicagoans, concerned about the poor quality of the city's public schools, are willing to pay more in taxes to improve them, a Tribune poll has found.

In addition, there is strong support among major Chicago-area businesses for a tax increase for the schools, especially if it is linked to improved student performance, according to a separate Tribune survey of top corporate leaders.

The school system has evolved, over the years, into a case of institutionalized child neglect because no one who has the political muscle has cared enough to force the schools to provide an adequate education. But the Tribune poll and survey findings, as well as other hopeful signs, such as the outcry of parents at the 19-day teachers' strike last fall, suggest that potent political forces in favor of school improvement may be coming together.

Politicians have long contended that a referendum to increase local property taxes would fail because most residents send their children to parochial schools or do not have children of school age. In addition, city and state business associations have consistently lobbied against tax increases for education.

Spokesman Robert Saigh said the School Board has not polled Chicagoans about a tax increase because "there were enough indications that it wouldn't be supported."

But the Tribune poll conducted in mid-February found that 56 percent of the Chicagoans surveyed said they would vote in favor of a referendum that would raise more money for the schools by increasing their taxes.

Thirty-seven percent said they would vote against the proposal, while 7 percent were not sure how they would vote.

"Is there anything better to spend your money on than education?" asks Henry Kutyna, 64, a bachelor in the West Ridge area on the Far North Side who said he would vote yes. "Education is a terrific thing."

Support for a tax increase was weakest among parents with children in private schools and among people who had no children. But even in these cases, the yes votes outnumbered the no votes by slight margins.

In the poll, 399 Chicagoans and 300 suburban residents were questioned on a wide range of education issues. The margin of error was 3.8 percentage points for the entire sample, 5 percentage points for Chicagoans, 6 percentage points for suburbanites and 7 percentage points for white Chicagoans or black Chicagoans.

Survey questionnaires were sent to the top executives of 100 businesses in Chicago and its suburbs, and 68 returned them. The group surveyed is not representative of business overall—some business lobbies continue their long opposition to school-tax increases—and is weighted toward major employers in a broad range of businesses.

Forty-one percent of the corporate leaders said they would vote for a school-tax increase if they could vote. Forty percent said they would vote no, and 18 percent were not sure.

"We support higher taxes," says Merrill Zenner, president of Reliable Corp., a privately held catalog house in Chicago that employs about 450 people and distributes office supplies.

"You'll get the money back because, if you get a better qualified person answering a job in the first place, they'll be easier and faster to train."

The approval rate was even greater in both the poll and survey when it was tied to a requirement that the schools improve student performance.

Asked about a referendum that would require more taxes only if the local schools improved student performance, two of three Chicagoans said they would vote yes and only 25 percent would vote no.

Business leaders were even stronger in their support on this question.

Nearly 74 percent said they would vote yes on such a proposal even if it would mean higher taxes for their companies. Only 13 percent said they would vote no, and 12 percent were not sure.

"I think business people believe we're underfunding education in Chicago," says Loren E. Smith, chairman and chief executive officer of Citicorp Savings of Illinois.

"Having said that, you don't dump a lot of money into guys who haven't done well with the money they've got in the past. You don't rearrange deck chairs on the Titanic."

The poll found also that Chicagoans want to have a greater say about who runs the schools and how.

For more than a century, the system has been run by a school board appointed by the mayor, but 52 percent of the Chicagoans polled said they would favor an elected board. Only 29 percent were opposed.

A major reason for the strong support for an elected board appears to be a feeling among residents of being locked out of school decisions. Three of 4 Chicagoans who expressed an opinion said they didn't have enough control over what goes on in the schools.

The poll and survey suggest that the money-starved system might be able to parlay the support for higher taxes into more funds.

More significantly, the findings suggest that citizens and businesses are willing to take responsibility for the schools—a responsibility that politicians have assiduously sought to avoid.

It is also a recognition of the economic threat that bad schools pose to the Chicago region if they cannot turn out enough qualified young people to meet the demands of the work force.

The corporate survey turned up a stunning measure of just how poorly the schools are doing in this regard.

Not even one of the 68 business leaders surveyed said the school system adequately prepared job applicants for work in entry-level jobs requiring less than a college education.

Tribune Poll ★

"How would you grade the average public school in Chicago?"

In percent

Grade	Chicagoans	Chicago whites	Chicago blacks	Suburbanites
A	1	0	3	0
B	13	5	25	4
C	35	32	39	21
D	26	33	17	26
F	11	16	5	10
Don't know	12	14	10	37
Avg. grade	**C-**	**D+**	**C**	**D+**

Margin of error: Chicagoans +/- 5 percentage points; whites and blacks, +/- 7; suburbanites, +/- 6

"How would you grade the average public school in the Chicago suburbs?"

In percent

Grade	Chicagoans	Chicago whites	Chicago blacks	Suburbanites
A	9%	7%	14%	7%
B	42	43	38	50
C	17	21	12	19
D	3	3	3	5
F	1	1	2	1
Don't know	28	26	31	18
Avg. grade	**B**	**B**	**B**	**B**

Margin of error: Chicagoans +/- 5 percentage points; whites and blacks, +/- 7; suburbanites, +/- 6

How Tribune poll was taken

Findings of the Tribune poll are based on interviews with 399 Chicagoans and 300 suburban residents selected by random-digit dialing from all Chicago-area households with telephones. The interviews were conducted from Feb. 11 through Feb. 19 by Market Share Inc., a market research firm.

The poll's margin of error is expected to be no more than 3.8 percentage points for the entire sample, 5 percentage points for Chicagoans, 6 percentage points for suburbanites, a 7 percentage pioints for white Chicagoans or black Chicagoans.

© The Chicago Tribune

And one of four said the applicants weren't prepared at all.

"We're simply appalled at what they can't do in the way of reading, writing and arithmetic," says John R. Conrad, president of S & C Electric Co.

The school system's failure has long exacted a human toll as its students have been unable to live up to their potential. It also has levied a high social cost in the form of greater welfare costs, higher crime and lost taxes.

"The thing we've got to focus on is the children," says R. Kenneth West, chairman of Harris Bank Corp. and a member of the executive committee of the mayor's education summit.

"We're not getting those children adequately educated, and it's desperate that we do so. Otherwise, we'll have disadvantaged kids growing into disadvantaged adults, and that's just not acceptable.

"These are people who aren't getting a chance. If they fail on their own, that's one thing. But, if they fail because we haven't given them an opportunity, that's our responsibility as citizens of this community.

"We can't blame anybody else."

The problems of the schools involve far more than just a lack of money.

Two of 3 Chicago students come from poor families. Seven of 8 are members of a racial or ethnic minority.

"The clients of the system are powerless," says James G. Ward, an assistant professor of educational administration at the University of Illinois, Urbana, who has conducted several studies of the Chicago public schools. "The people who really care about this system don't tend to vote, don't tend to be parts of powerful groups."

Nonetheless, the Tribune poll found that people who had voted in the last two years were stronger in their support of a school tax increase than people who said they hadn't voted.

Of course, it is one thing for a person to tell a pollster that he'd vote for a tax increase and another to actually do it. One factor the poll could not take into account is that public opinion is invariably changed by the campaigns mounted by proponents and opponents of a real ballot proposition. The matter is further complicated because Chicagoans haven't had a chance to vote on a school referendum in two decades.

Only 13 percent of the students in the public schools are white, but 48 percent of the white Chicagoans polled said they would favor a tax increase; 45 percent would oppose such a proposal. Blacks in the city favored a tax increase 67 percent to 27 percent.

If the tax increase were accompanied by a guarantee of improved student performance, whites would approve the measure 2-to-1, and blacks 5-to-1.

Linda Burkes, the mother of two public school students, was one of many blacks to favor increased funding.

"When I was in public school, the teachers were much better, they were stricter, and they cared," says Burkes, 33, whose husband teaches in a private alternative education program.

Burkes has done volunteer work in many South Side schools and says she has seen much to persuade her that the schools need improvement. At Kenwood Academy, 5015 S. Blackstone Ave., for example, she met a counselor who had a poem tacked on his wall bemoaning the quality of the students. She ran into a similar attitude at

Du Sable High School, 4934 S. Wabash Ave.

"All I heard from the teachers at Du Sable was how illiterate the kids are and how bad," Burkes recalls. "I heard nothing but negative things about the kids. If there wasn't a law, I'd keep my kids home and teach them myself."

Most white Chicagoans are highly critical of the public schools, but many of those who oppose a tax increase say money isn't the problem.

"They're wasting all the money," says Genevieve Rodak, 73, of the South Chicago neighborhood, who put her two children through the public schools more than 30 years ago. "I went to public school. My kids went to public school. We got a good education, but today they don't want to. I don't blame the schools. I blame the kids because they don't want to learn."

From the start of public education in Chicago in 1834, public schools have been the poor relations of the political establishment. They have been used by political leaders as a source of patronage and contracts. Education of the children— particularly poor children—has been of secondary importance.

The system has been a fiefdom of City Hall, with politicians exercising indirect control without fear of being held accountable for the failure of the schools.

In some cities, such as New York, public schools are part of the municipal government and are the direct responsibility of the mayor. In most Illinois communities, local school systems are separate governmental bodies run by elected school boards.

In Chicago, the school system is a separate government but not answerable to the voters. The 11 members of the Chicago Board of Education are appointed, and as a result voters have no direct way to express their pleasure or displeasure.

This political isolation has been increased over the last two decades by the refusal of school officials—and City Hall—to propose tax increases to the voters.

Such wasn't always the case. In 1967, for example, a 15-cent increase per $100 assessed valuation was approved 63 percent to 37 percent.

A year later, another 15-cent increase —which had the backing of the Chicago Teachers Union, the business community and Mayor Richard J. Daley—was approved 52 to 48.

Since then, the people of Chicago haven't been asked to raise their own taxes. Even so, the school tax rate has increased by 49 percent since 1968.

Those "backdoor" school tax increases were approved by the legislature.

"What do [the state legislators] care?" says George Munoz, a school board member and former board president. "They're approving it for Chicago. They don't have to pay for it."

But Ald. Edwin Eisendrath (43d), a former teacher finishing his first year on the council, says: "I don't think it's fair to go to Springfield to increase local property taxes. It takes the burden off the Board of Education. It takes the burden off the mayor.

"It would have been so much better —so much more honest—if we had a school board, with a product that the people would support, say, 'Let's go to a referendum.'

"They haven't had the courage to do it."

System flunks test of public opinion

The top leaders of the Chicago public school system award themselves high marks and say the schools are improving. Mayor Eugene Sawyer agrees.

But Chicagoans, suburbanites and business leaders throughout the metropolitan area strongly disagree.

They give the system low grades and contend that it is getting worse, according to the results of a Tribune poll of 699 city and suburban residents and a Tribune survey of top executives of 68 of the Chicago area's leading employers.

School Supt. Manford Byrd Jr., who has held a variety of other high-ranking posts in 34 years in the city schools, says he deserves a B or B-plus for his work as superintendent since 1985.

"In terms of the achievement of the youngsters, it's better than it was as measured by test scores," Byrd says. "There has been some movement. When you put it up against the backdrop of where we should be, there's a ways to go."

Frank W. Gardner, president of the school board and a former teacher and principal in the school system, gives himself and the school board high marks.

"This board, as I experience it, really has encouraged me because it is a working board, a very dedicated board," he says. "If you measure relative to reaching our goals, we have not reached our goals so I would say a B because we have not reached our goals. It's not for lack of effort."

Sawyer, speaking at an April 8 conference sponsored by the Chicago Urban League and Northwestern University, gave Byrd and the school board a B, although he criticized the school system's "self-perpetuating" bureaucracy. Later, he noted that others would give the school leadership an even higher mark.

But those who participated in the Tribune poll were not so generous. Only 1 of 7 Chicagoans, and only 1 of every 25 suburbanites, was willing to give the city schools an A or a B.

Instead, the average Chicagoan gave the school system a C-minus and the average suburbanite gave it a D-plus. (In contrast, Chicagoans and suburbanites gave the average suburban school a B.)

The business leaders were even more pessimistic.

Not one of the 68 gave the schools an A or a B, and nearly 1 in 4 flunked the system. The average grade was a low D. (In comparison, nearly 3 of 4 of the surveyed executives gave the average suburban school an A or B.)

But, as low as the grades for the city

Report card: *School Supt. Manford Byrd Jr. (left) and Frank W. Gardner, school board president, give themselves high marks.*

schools are, they may not have hit bottom.

The Tribune poll found that 43 percent of city and suburban residents believe that the system has gotten worse in recent years while only 11 percent had seen improvement. Three of every 4 suburbanites—and 9 of every 10 Chicago whites—who had perceived a change said the system was declining.

The business leaders, again, were even more pessimistic. Two of every 3 who expressed an opinion said the schools were getting worse. Only 1 of the 68 company leaders surveyed said he's seen any improvement in the system.

Black Chicagoans generally gave the public schools higher marks than whites.

Nonetheless, 3 of 4 black public school parents said they would send their children to a private or parochial school if they could afford to, and nearly 2 of 3 said they would move to a better school system if they had the money to do so.

Although U.S. Education Secretary William Bennett didn't take part in the poll or survey, he expressed his ranking of the Chicago public schools last fall when he called them the worst in the nation.

Byrd and other school and civic leaders took a rosier view.

The schools, Byrd said, aren't the worst—only the sixth worst of the 21 largest districts where the American College Test is given.

What's ahead? *Kindergarteners at Goudy Elementary School, the class of 2000: Business leaders fear a shortage of qualified workers by then.*

Too many graduates can't make it in the workplace

Education 'represents Chicago's Achilles heel'

'**F**or 40 years we have been employing high school graduates from the Chicago Public Schools," said Dempsey Travis, his voice quivering with anger. "But something has happened in the last two decades I don't understand."

Until this moment, it had been one of those business-as-usual meetings. Chicago school principals had asked local business leaders to address their annual conference on what business could do for the public schools and vice versa.

But the polite calm disappeared when Travis—owner of a South Side real estate firm, author of books on real estate, jazz and black politics in Chicago, and a 1939 graduate of Du Sable High School—stood up to address the more than 200 principals who attended the March meeting.

Travis waved 70 applications in the air. His firm needed two secretary-receptionists, he said, but he had to screen 70 high school graduates before he could find two who were qualified.

"This to me is an indictment," he told the school leaders.

If what Travis described is criminal, the schools are on a spree. Horror stories abound—at a bank, for example, where more than three-quarters of the applicants for entry-level jobs cannot fill out the job application; at a machine shop, where parades of young applicants don't know how many 16ths there are in an inch.

So far, businesses have been able to sort through the legions of unqualified applicants to find enough acceptable people for job openings.

But unless there is a dramatic turnaround in the quality of city schools, the situation threatens to undermine the prosperity of the entire Chicago region, according to experts interviewed in the Tribune's seven-month examination of the school system.

Indeed, there is a growing fear that before the turn of the 21st Century, only a dozen years from now, the Chicago region—city and suburbs alike—will be stricken by a shortage of qualified entry-level people.

"We're competing for business and economic opportunity with countries around the world as well as cities around the country," said Peter S. Willmott, chairman of Carson Pirie Scott & Co. "If we continue to have a functionally illiterate and uneducated group coming out of the high schools, we'll become a Third World city. We won't be a world-class city unless we have an educated, aware work force."

Chicago and other older urban centers with large populations of impoverished people are at a severe disadvantage in this economic opportunity sweepstakes because of three powerful trends that are starting to collide:

• The number of young workers entering the work force each year is rapidly declining. The entire Baby Boom generation has entered the job market. Now it's the Baby Bust's turn.

• In the Chicago region and areas like it, a growing proportion of this shrinking entry-level labor pool comes from impoverished backgrounds and suffers the consequences of inadequate education. Employers report over and over again that they see a steady stream of graduates and dropouts from Chicago schools who are unqualified for even the most menial jobs.

• The relentless advance of workplace technology is demanding that these workers have ever greater skills, ruling out more and more people who are now marginally employable.

Despite increasingly strident warnings from the business community about the coming crunch, the public school system each year graduates, drops out or pushes out another class of non-college-bound youth largely ill-prepared for the rapidly changing world of work.

The social costs of this bankrupt educational enterprise can be measured in high unemployment, welfare dependency, increased crime and reduced income. These costs not only take a terrible human toll, but affect every taxpayer by causing ever higher city and state taxes to support the services needed to cope with these problems. Bad schools also drive middle-class taxpayers from the city, leaving fewer people to pay the tax.

The social costs also sap the economy. The Chicago Panel on Public School Policy and Finance, an education watchdog group, estimated in 1985 that the 12,600 students who dropped out of the class of 1982 earned 19 percent less than the average high school graduate, an annual loss of $39.8 million in regional buying power. Moreover, they paid $7.3 million less in federal and state income taxes and cost the government an additional $50.2 million in unemployment and welfare payments compared to high school graduates.

And for business, the bill for long-term neglect of the city's public education system has finally come due:

• In a Tribune survey of 68 top business leaders, not one city or suburban business reported that its entry-level applicants from Chicago schools were adequately prepared for work. Pinstripe frustration with the high school graduates stretches beyond the city limits, since many suburban businesses rely on city residents to fill entry-level and lower-skilled positions.

• Businesses throughout the area struggle with thousands of applications from unqualified candidates. Some are instituting tests to screen out applicants whose high school diplomas don't translate into a grasp of math and reading.

• The number of companies taking on the cost of in-house basic education courses is rising rapidly. Technological advances make it necessary to teach their current workers—including many recent high school graduates—basic skills they never learned in school.

The devalued status of a diploma from Chicago schools was documented by the Mayor's Office of Employment and Training last year. The job-training agency tested 771 of the 25,000 students and recent graduates in its summer job program. The average reading score for high school graduates was 8th grade. Fully 25 percent tested below the 6th-grade level.

This educational failure is adding to the cost of doing business, and peering into the future gives business leaders the jitters.

"If only 40 percent graduate and only 12 percent are educated at the full high school level," said Loren Smith, chairman of Citicorp Savings of Illinois, "we're very concerned about whether we'll find the qualified people we need."

Smith's concern isn't theoretical. His firm is being inundated by unqualified applicants. Citicorp gets 1,000 applications a week for its teller and clerk slots. Yet 84 percent are rejected out of hand because the applicants can't complete the form, according to a personnel officer.

The failure of the schools will not only hurt existing business, but it may doom the effort to revive lagging parts of the city's economy. This is especially true in economically decimated sections of the South, Southeast and West Sides.

Education " represents Chicago's Achilles heel," said Robert M. Ady, vice president of the Fantus Company, the nation's leading industrial location firm. "Workers have to be able to think on their feet. The days of the human robot are gone. The implications for education are profound."

A Fantus study for the Illinois Department of Commerce and Community Affairs in 1986 pointed out that regional differences in the cost of doing business have narrowed significantly in the past decade. It said the chief concern of businesses today in deciding where to locate facilities is "the quality and trainability of the work force."

School officials bristle at the charge that they are turning out a product ill-suited to the needs of business. "That simply is not borne out by the tests that have been given," School Supt. Manford Byrd Jr. said of his graduates. "The information we're getting is that they are getting better, not worse."

Byrd suggested that employer problems with Chicago high school graduates are related to young people's work attitudes—their ability to show up on time, dress appropriately and show enthusiasm for work—and not to their reading and math proficiency.

He and others interviewed also suggested that high dropout rates were caused in part by the failure of the local economy to provide enough jobs.

"Students look around, particularly minority students, at their brothers and friends and see extraordinary unemployment rates, or they're in jobs that pay minimum wage and aren't enough to raise a family," said Richard Murnane of the Harvard Graduate School of Education. "Where are the incentives to work hard in school?"

However, the economic prospects for inner-city youths are improving. The economy is expanding while fewer young people are entering the job market.

Indeed, business leaders, demographers and job training experts suggest that the groups left out of the general prosperity of recent years have their best chance in decades for moving into the economic mainstream.

Between 1985 and 2000, the population of Cook County between the ages of 15 and 24 will shrink 18 percent, according to the Illinois Bureau of the Budget. For the first time, a majority of these young adults will be black and Hispanic. By 2000, minorities in Cook County will comprise 53.1 percent of the 15-to-24-year-old age group, up from 43.8 percent in 1985.

This minority makeup of the next generation of entry-level workers is significant because a large proportion of blacks and Hispanics come from impoverished backgrounds, are concentrated in the Chicago schools and, as a result, are more likely to finish their school careers without the skills the job market requires.

At the same time, businesses will be asking young workers to perform jobs that are being transformed by new technology. According to labor market analysts, the academic and thinking skills needed on the job will rise dramatically.

Service and information-based industries, which require much higher levels of reading, writing, communication and mathematical skills than the stagnant manufacturing sector, will continue to grow. Remaining manufacturing jobs will require greater skills because of modernization.

"Workers will be expected to read and understand directions, add and subtract, and be able to speak and think clearly," the Hudson Institute reported last year in its Workforce 2000 study for the U.S. Department of Labor. "In other words, jobs that are currently in the middle of the skill distribution will be the least-skilled occupations of the future, and there will be very few net new jobs for the unskilled."

Most local businesses until very recently ignored a Chicago school system that turned out large numbers of people, including many with diplomas, who were virtually unemployable. As international competition cut deeply into once-robust manufacturing companies, many businesses were laying off workers instead of looking for new ones.

Even in service businesses that were expanding, employers could pick and choose workers from the multitude of Baby Boomers and women entering the workforce. Laid-off factory workers added to the crowds of job-seekers.

But these sources of new workers are drying up. Employers soon will have to hire extensively from the Baby Bust generation.

"With the shrinking of our industrial base, there was a surplus of skilled people," said Ronald J. Gidwitz, chairman of Helene Curtis Industries Inc. and chairman of the city's Economic Development Commission. "In 5 or 10 years, we won't have that."

Complaints about the quality of public school graduates from elite business groups, corporate lobbyists and local employers have been escalating. But beyond token projects by individual businesses with a single school—the Adopt-A-School program—or an occasional blue-ribbon study, the business community has done little to change the situation.

"We were not sufficiently alarmed,"

said B. Kenneth West, chairman of the Harris Trust and Savings Bank and a recent recruit to school reform efforts. "It was not perceived as business' primary responsibility."

Now some corporations are moving to fund experimental vocational and antidropout programs. Some business leaders are working with community and parent groups in the wake of last year's 19-day teachers' strike.

There are even signs that business opposition to a school tax increase may be softening. A Tribune survey of top local business leaders found that a substantial majority would support higher taxes if the money were tied to better performance from the schools.

The cost of a poorly educated workforce recently hit home at Handy Button Machine Co., 1750 N. 25th Ave., Melrose Park. Last year, General Motors Corp. threatened to stop doing business with parts suppliers that didn't adopt a Japanese-style quality control system called statistical process control. It requires 8th-grade math skills.

Handy Button, which makes upholstery buttons for the auto giant, wanted to adopt the new system quickly. But the company, which moved out of the Pilsen neighborhood on the West Side in 1980 and still draws most of its workers from the city, made a disturbing discovery. Many of its workers didn't have the needed math skills, so it had to start a training program.

"The people who graduate from Chicago's schools, their knowledge is totally inadequate," said Lenard Baritz, president of Handy Button. "We have to teach people what the schools haven't

taught them."

This growing need for basic skills on the job cuts across all sectors of the economy. Throughout the manufacturing sector, good-paying jobs that require mechanical skills but not much in the way of academic and thinking skills are disappearing rapidly. As plants modernize—which they have to do to survive in the competitive global economy—the jobs that remain call for skills like the ones being taught at Handy Button.

Meanwhile, service occupations, which accounted for virtually all new jobs in the last 10 years, are expected to continue growing rapidly. More than 90 percent of the 269,000 new jobs that will be created in Cook County between 1984 and 1995 will be in services, according to new projections from the Illinois Department of Employment Security.

Many of these jobs will require significant post-high school training. Projected fast-growing fields include registered nurses, accountants, computer programmers and teachers.

But even in service industries that create a large number of low-paid slots —cashiers, secretaries, janitors, waiters, guards and general office clerks are among the high-growth occupations—the new jobs call for higher levels of reading, writing and mathematical skills than the manufacturing jobs they are replacing.

"Of the new jobs generated, 37 percent will require high skill, 56 percent will be in the middle-range of skills and only 2 percent will be low-skilled jobs," said Chris Reynolds of the Illinois Department of Commerce and Community Affairs. By 1995, only 1 Chicago area worker in 10 will be in a low-skilled position, down from 17 percent currently and 22 percent in 1970.

The results of these historic shifts are already being felt. Some firms are starting basic education programs for their workers because they don't have the skills needed for the changing nature of work.

Last April, Nabisco Brands Inc.'s 3,000-employee bakery at 7300 S. Kedzie Ave. began offering free afternoon classes to upgrade the reading and math skills of employees.

"We are introducing computers on the floor that require higher levels of skill," said Nancy Cobb, human resource development manager at Nabisco. "The process control equipment will require the ability to read computer screens and monitor the data."

Ten employers in the Northwest suburbs, including Motorola Corp., Alexian Brothers Hospital in Elk Grove and the Marriott Hotel in Schaumburg, have asked William Rainey Harper College to set up similar programs. "We've seen quite an interest in this program over the past year," said Patricia Mulcrone, chairman of adult educational development at the college. "There is a large workforce of semiskilled workers not ready for jobs of the future unless we teach basic skills."

Many firms in growth industries have started giving applicants reading and math tests to see if high school graduates actually learned anything in school.

The Chicago Board Options Exchange, for instance, gives a fractions test to people applying for entry-level price-reporting and quote-reporting positions. The jobs, 68 percent of which are held by city residents, entail recording prices into a computer. The jobs are considered a good place to get started in the futures and options business.

But to hire 150 people last year, the CBOE had to test 425 high school graduates, only 53 percent of whom passed. "It's incredible how many people can't pass the test," said Rory Zaks, assistant vice president for human resources at the CBOE. "Those fractions are critical to our functioning."

As the needs of employers continue to expand, the shrinking pool of entry-level workers suggest a turnaround could be at hand for those who were left out of the past decade's prosperity.

But there is a catch. The jobs will go only to those with an adequate education.

"The demographic reality for the 16-to-24 age group today is that if he does well in school and gets trained, he can get a good job," said Anthony Carnevale, chief economist for the American Society of Training and Development. "There are opportunities for the minority and disadvantaged population that simply didn't exist in the 1970s and early 1980s.

"The problem," he said, "is we're having a hard time communicating this to people."

Keep out: *A Du Sable teacher locks her supply cabinet in response to burglaries. One teacher has been robbed twice while leaving school.*

Sea of students: *It's between periods at Manley, a neighborhood high school with a limited curriculum and limited supplies.*

Selection system
can make the cruelest cut of all

'They are the children
of a lesser God'

T he majority of Chicago high school students are consigned to dilapidated, mostly segregated neighborhood schools serving a course of study that prepares them neither for college nor the world of work.

They are the discards in a three-tiered system of wildly inconsistent quality, a system of educational triage that results in a separate and unequal education for the city's 111,891 high school students.

Those the system chooses to save are the brightest youngsters, selected by race, income and achievement for academic and vocational magnet schools where teachers are hand-picked and supplies are plentiful.

The remaining 66,371 students are tagged with third-class status and sent to neighborhood schools where a limited curriculum and the lack of supplies stand as a daily reminder of their shortcomings.

Most of these students do not go on to college. Yet they are fed a steady diet of academic subjects designed for college-bound students.

Most do poorly. A majority drop out. Few leave school with a good grasp of even the basic reading and math skills looked for by employers or colleges.

A third of the class of 1985 were unemployed a year after graduation, a study for the mayor's education summit found. Another third were in college and a third were working.

Selective academic schools such as Whitney Young Magnet High and Lane Technical High make up the top tier and operate much like private institutions, accepting only students with solid attendance records, excellent grades and above average standardized test scores.

More than 20,000 of the system's best students are channeled into 12 selective high schools. Another 11,760 attend community academies that offer some special programs to students who live in the school's enrollment area.

Chicago's academic magnet schools were created as a result of a desegregation lawsuit. But in a system whose students are overwhelmingly black and Hispanic, the separation of the best from the rest has spawned a different kind of segregation that discriminates on the basis of achievement as well as race.

Students who cannot get into the top schools but want a decent preparation for college compete for spots in selective vocational schools that offer academic as well as technical training.

Those schools, set up to groom students with no college plans, have become second choice as havens for college-bound students who might otherwise flee the crumbling city schools.

The selective vocational schools have become the middle tier between the elite college preparatory schools and the neighborhood schools. About 11,000 students attend five selective vocational high schools. Another 1,876 attend vocational schools that do not select students on the basis of achievement.

"A high percentage of the kids here aren't interested in vocational education," said Jack Perlin, principal of Prosser Vocational High, 2148 N. Long Ave. "They come here because it's perceived as a safe place."

The 39 neighborhood schools make up the bottom tier, the place where students land when they can go nowhere else.

"The effect on students who do not go to school with high achievers is devastating," said Alvin Lubov, principal of Douglass Middle School, 543 N. Waller Ave. "It's hard to overcome feelings of rejection."

"It anoints certain youngsters," said Jack Mitchell, field superintendent for high schools. "Their whole attitude is changed. [Those who aren't selected]

are leftovers. "They are the children of a lesser God."

The academic magnets and vocational schools have not only the best students but also the most involved parents and the best of the teaching staff.

"There is a great deal of pressure on our teachers because 50 percent of our parents are college graduates," said Powhatan Collins, principal of Whitney Young, 211 S. Laflin St. "They know what it takes for a child to get into a top college, and if we're not doing it, we hear about it."

Meanwhile, low-achieving students who enter neighborhood high schools must take double and triple sessions of remedial classes to meet tougher city and state mandates for graduation.

As a result, few have time to take vocational or business electives that would prepare them for work, or art and music classes that might spark their interest in learning and, perhaps, keep them in school.

"Students have to pass the requisites to graduate," said Kenneth Van Spankeren, principal of Orr High, 730 N.

Pulaski Rd. "Those core subjects take up most of their time."

"They're taking two periods of English or math," said Harry Tobin, director of vocational education for the system. "So it shrinks the number of opportunities for a student to take electives like vocational education."

Ironically, the vocational courses the students cannot fit into their schedule might help them learn academic subjects.

"Teaching basic math is part of our curriculum," said Theoda Smith, a plumbing teacher at Dunbar. "About 3 percent of the kids have basic math problems. But I haven't failed yet in teaching them how to use fractions. They learn when it's hands-on."

Yet, despite their advantages in reaching slow learners, vocational courses have been trimmed from general schools due to budget cuts.

The electronics shop was dropped at Orr in 1985. A school radio station died four years ago. A commercial art class was canceled this year.

The pressure to maintain the triple-tiered system is intense. Academic magnet and selective vocational schools are the only remaining hold the school system has on the middle class in Chicago.

"I stayed in Chicago because my daughter's [magnet] school is a good one," said Jody Baty, member of the Parents United to Reform Education, who testified at a joint legislative hearing in the fall. "We would not have stayed if we could go only to our local school."

But magnet schools have triggered resentment in the parents of students who are overlooked. They complain that the magnets drain the system's best teachers and scarce resources.

"We're tired of hearing everyone complain about how the layoffs might affect the precious magnet schools," said Denise Brown, a South Side parent, when it was thought that cutbacks after the fall teacher strike might affect the magnets.

"Why haven't these people complained about the way our children are treated in the neighborhood schools? It's because they don't care about the children in the neighborhood schools."

Charting the past: *Herbert Tarnor uses a 1962 periodic table in a Du Sable chemistry class. Six new elements are not on the chart.*

Corn popper, soda bottles: Elements of a chemistry class

'Can't you see I'm busy
playing cards here?'

A child walks in the door of a public high school.

What is he offered? What opportunities does she have?

It depends.

In Chicago, it depends on whether the school is attended primarily by black and Hispanic students or white and Asian students.

It depends on whether the school is a magnet or competitive vocational school—designed to draw the top students—or a neighborhood school, for teenagers who can't go anywhere else.

And it depends upon the income of the students' parents and where they live, making a lie of the promise that education is the door to opportunity.

As part of a seven-month examination of Chicago Public Schools, Tribune reporters visited high schools throughout the city. The contrasts were stark. This is a walk through those schools.

The periodic table hanging on the wall of the chemistry laboratory in Du Sable High is dated 1962.

It is torn and stained and contains only 103 elements, with no indication that six more have been discovered in the quarter-century since. The false ceiling in the room has collapsed and wires are hanging down. The laboratory floor—rotted by a flood seven months before and now buckled down to the subfloor—cannot be walked on in certain spots.

Teacher Herbert Tarnor ticks off the equipment he is lacking—beakers, distillation equipment, cold water, bunsen burners. He uses a popcorn popper to heat experiments. He cuts plastic soda bottles for supplies—shallow ones for petri dishes, taller ones for beakers.

New equipment that was to have been provided with Build Illinois funds hasn't arrived at Du Sable, an all-black neighborhood school at 4934 S. Wabash Ave.

"There are many experiments that we simply cannot do," Tarnor says. "The students are better motivated than many I have seen. But this school has been underfunded for some time."

Amanda Wolfe, 14, is measuring water in a graduated cylinder, waiting her turn to use one of the three polariscopes in the earth science laboratory at Whitney Young, an academic magnet school at 211 S. Laflin St.

Today's assignment is to identify a mineral specimen, and to do that, Amanda must examine the physical and chemical properties of her "mystery rock."

"We have to feel the texture, things like that," she said. The students also must look at the rock through polarized light.

Equipment abounds in the laboratory. Students work with pipettes, sophisticated centrifuges and balances accurate to a fraction of a milligram.

Amanda is here because she is bright, and because her mother insisted that she overcome her anxiety and compete with the best in a magnet school rather than going to her neighborhood high school.

Mario Williams, 14, describes to teacher Harriette Manuel the math he used to determine the specific gravity (ratio of the weight of a substance to the weight of an equal volume of water) of his rock and the experiment he did to prove it.

"I was only off by 45 one-hundredths," he says proudly.

"Excellent!" Manuel says, giving Mario a pat on the shoulder. "I can pull this kind of thinking out of these students," she says. "I know they have it in them."

Willie Reavers, 16, sits in a study hall at Bowen High, 2710 E. 89th St., and works on an unusual math project.

"Don't bother me, man," Willie tells his cousin, Calvin Reavers, 15, as he adds the points for the Queen of Spades, the 7 of Diamonds and the King and Queen of Hearts. "Can't you see I'm busy playing cards here? You're going to break my concentration."

Willie's schedule includes two study halls every day. Calvin's schedule includes three. They use the time to play 52 Pickup, Gin Rummy, Pitty Pat or Hearts. Bowen, a neighborhood school, has an enrollment that is about half black and half Hispanic.

"Sometimes I read the paper or talk to my friends or just chill out, but I usually play cards," Willie said.

"Not much studying goes on in study hall," said Tim Tuten, a history teacher who is minding the study hall. "I let the students play cards because I figure they might get some math skills out of it. I just don't allow them to gamble."

It is 7 a.m. A group of 21 Sullivan High School students are already in class, holding a robust debate on whether a leader can be truly moral in a less than perfect world. The focus is on Lycurgus, founder of the Commonwealth of Sparta in ancient Greece.

"If we are really talking about power, then morals aren't important," says student Doug Funke. "What makes you powerful is when you are loved and feared at the same time. That's why gang leaders and dictators are so powerful. They make people love them, and then they strike fear in their hearts."

The class erupts in a cacophony of conflicting opinions until Sullivan Principal Robert Brazil asks, "Was Lycurgus' commonwealth a democratic or communist society?"

The class explodes in conversation again. Sullivan, 6631 N. Bosworth Ave., is a relatively affluent, integrated neighborhood high school.

"The program is an outlet for children who might not be stimulated by a more traditional curriculum," Brazil said. "Some kids who are very bright cannot survive in our education system because it is too limiting.

"Some people think that Chicago Public School children can't learn. I wish those people could see these kids."

Hubbard High Principal Charles Vietzen walks through a production technology class and moves his hand along a new piece of equipment that resembles a two-sided telephone booth.

Inside the carrel, a student drops a cassette into a wall-mounted tape player and listens to step-by-step instructions on how to install electrical wiring. Students elsewhere in the room get detailed lessons in robotics, plumbing, carpentry, tile setting and basic telephone installation.

"This is the class they used to call wood shop, where kids would make bookends and wastebaskets," Vietzen says. "The problem was that it didn't train students for a job. We now have the equipment to teach them how to build a product, taking it through all the steps of mass production from start to finish."

Hubbard, a neighborhood school at 6200 S. Hamlin Ave., with a magnet program and a 53.7 percent minority enrollment, received $67,000 worth of new equipment this year, including such exotic improvements as a dust-free room for the robotics equipment.

They've really got some kind of program," says Fred Kane, Chicago's vocational education coordinator. "It's really too bad that every school in the city can't have equipment like this."

King Collier spent 16 weeks in an auto shop class at Du Sable before he learned how to change a tire—a skill normally taught in the first week of class.

King's first shop teacher, Albert Isaac, took a leave of absence at the beginning of the school year. The parade of substitutes assigned to take Isaac's place were not insured against injury or certified to teach the class. As a result, they could not enter the shop or touch the cars.

One substitute, according to students, slept his way through most of the first semester.

"The substitute would come in and he'd say, 'Read your book. You can talk, just keep it down,' " said senior Michael Ivory. "Pretty soon, you'd look up and he be sleeping."

Willie Jackson, a certified shop teacher, was assigned to the class four weeks before the end of the first semester.

Mixing water and wood: Chemistry students at Du Sable must step lightly as a result of a flood that buckled the floor and made it unsafe for walking.

"This class is lost," Jackson said. "By now they should be able to fix a radiator leak, do a brake job. But first we have to try to get this shop in order. It really looks like a junkyard. It's almost too dangerous for the kids."

"We could have really used a class like this," King, 17, said. "Let's be real. Most of us ain't going to college. If we would have learned something in here, we could have used it to help us get a job. As it is, it was just a waste of our time."

Inside the main office at Phillips High, an all-black school at 244 E. Pershing Rd., Principal Ernestine Curry and her staff face myriad morning problems. Among them is a girl who wants to enroll in high school.

The girl's mother explains that her daughter, 14, is pregnant. "They wanted to put her in 8th grade, but she's a 9th grader."

The child sits silently next to her mother, sucking her thumb.

It's third period study hall for George Washington, 17, a senior at Dunbar Vocational High, 3000 S. King Dr.

But instead of wasting the hour, he trots down to the architectural drawing lab to work on his axonometric (three-sided) projection of a beach house for the Museum of Science and Industry's architectural drawing competition.

"I've worked on it for 2½ weeks," he says. "I come in here during my lunch period."

Such dedication isn't exceptional, according to Robert Heersema, who's taught the class for 15 years at Dunbar. "Most of the students in here plan to go to college, and most plan to major in architecture," he said.

The 33 students majoring in architecture, one of 25 vocational choices at Dunbar, get a three-hour daily dose of drawing, using the same text that's used in freshman drafting courses at the University of Illinois-Chicago campus, according to Heersema.

"When my kids get to college, the drafting courses are a breeze," he said.

More than half of the toilets in the first floor girls' washrooms at Manley High, 2935 W. Polk St., are unusable—stopped up, boarded over. Graffiti everywhere. There are no doors on most of the stalls. There is no toilet paper or paper towels.

The number of broken toilets is higher than in most Chicago high schools, but the absence of supplies is not typical.

"The students use the paper to plug up the sinks and toilets," explained Principal Judith Steinhagen of Du Sable. She said she feared that students might break glass mirrors and "use the shards for weapons."

Every day at 8th period, about 14 teenagers at Manley close the door of a corner room on the third floor—shutting out the fights and the shrieks in the hallway—and, under dirty skylights and bug-ridden fluorescent fixtures, make music.

They open their cases, take out the shiny instruments and fill the air with cool blues and hot jazz.

It wasn't always like this. When teacher William Wisniewski arrived at Manley a few years ago, there were so few instruments that, he said, "the students not only had to share horns, they had to share mouthpieces."

With money tight and many students subsisting on welfare, Wisniewski decided to concentrate on a jazz band rather than the traditional marching band. "That way I don't have to buy uniforms," he said. "And one tuba would wipe out my entire budget."

Students in the band have reading scores that range from very low to average against national standards. But the music, Wisniewski says, motivates them, makes them competitive. Last year they took third place in the Midwest Jazz Band Festival. A neighborhood school, Manley's enrollment is all black, mostly poor.

Sylvester Powell and his brother, Amherst, play first and second trumpet.

No marching: *With money tight, a jazz band makes more sense than a marching band at Manley High.*

"I've been playing seven years," says Sylvester. Using his brother's nickname, he says, "I picked up A-love's trumpet and just started playing it."

During "Birdland," Antonio Burris, 16, works his snare drum and high hat cymbal in complex syncopated rhythms while the saxophones trade the melody line with the trumpets.

At the end, Wisniewski is pleased. "We have two concerts next week. You're almost ready."

Joe Armistead's teacher at Du Sable insists that he can be anything that he wants to be.

Joe disagrees.

But not because he lacks intelligence or drive. The 17-year-old is a B student and plans to join the service after he graduates in June. His lack of confidence stems from his inability to get into one of the exclusive magnet, technical or vocational programs.

"What if I want to be a scientist?" Joe said, in a discussion with his classmates, many of whom live in the Robert Taylor Homes public housing project.

"How can I even hope to be a scientist when my school has old and rotting science labs and there isn't even enough equipment to go around? They put the best students in the best schools with the best teachers and leave the rest of us in broken-up buildings where we barely have enough books.

"If you're not in a magnet school, it's like you don't count."

At the end of the discussion, Joe is asked to give an example of segregation. He lifts his lanky frame out of his desk and points to a Chicago school board poster on the wall.

"Our schools be the biggest example of segregation I've seen."

Student, Teacher: *Eighth grader Chanel Branch, 14, shares a book at home with her 14-month-old son.*

8th-grade graduates
take along dreams and little else

*'Some do not know
their multiplication tables'*

Fifty-five ribbons will be handed out this year at Goudy Elementary, silken tokens to be worn like badges of honor during the last few days of school. The girls pin them to their blouses. Boys fasten them to their pants.

The children wear them as a prelude to their 8th-grade graduation in June. They signify the end of the formative years that a child spends in the Chicago Public School system. The end of elementary school, where the underpinnings of failure are often firmly established, where a child is either turned on to the idea of an education or forever lost.

Over the course of a seven-month examination of the Chicago Public Schools, The Tribune spent time with the students who are a part of Goudy's Class of 1988.

These are some of the children Goudy will send on to high school:

There's Chanel Branch, who after a fight with a girlfriend came to school with her cheeks carved up with scratch marks. She is 14, on welfare, and the mother of a 14-month-old son.

Marc Venton took the initiative to apply to Sullivan High School. But he was not accepted. "He hurt himself," said Barbara Boxton, Goudy's school counselor, who said she understands that he was turned down largely because of his attitude during a personal interview at the school.

Ronald Sims has already joined a neighborhood street gang. "It was stupid," he explains. Yet, he wears his gold earring to flaunt his membership most every day. He points to the mark under an eye, a scar he said he received during his mandatory initiation "violation," 40 hits with bats and sticks. He says he won't subject himself to another 40 hits required for a safe passage out of the gang.

Delia Avila, who said her family speaks only Spanish, has learned English at Goudy. Her teachers say she has made great strides. This year, she reads from a 4th-grade book.

Myreon Flowers has been tested to read poorer than the average 3d-grader. But he has moved from 7th to 8th grade halfway through the school year because Goudy is strict about following the Board of Education policy that a child, often regardless of academic accomplishment, should be promoted out of elementary school in the year he turns 15.

At the top of the class is Hector Ayala, a soft-spoken boy who wears dark-rimmed glasses. He is called "the smart one" by his peers. First marking period, he received an A in language arts, A+ in math. He liked "Animal Farm," one of the novels he has read this year.

Bobby Brantley is also in 8th grade. But he refuses to sit in teacher Bernice Eiland's class.

So he walks the hallways. Runs errands for teachers. Reads movie star magazines and listens to his Walkman while sitting in the school's behavior-disorder classroom because he likes that teacher. Occasionally, he just leaves the building and says he is going home to watch TV.

He, too, will graduate.

Halfway through the school year, only six of the prospective 8th-grade graduates at Goudy, 5120 N. Winthrop Ave., were considered by their teachers to be performing on an academic level that is expected in 8th grade. Both teachers report that more children are doing better now.

Nearly all have received check marks on their report cards indicating that they need to exercise more self-control.

But if the ribbons will signify anything, it is that none of these things really matter, at least not where 8th-grade graduation is concerned.

What matters is the child's age. That and the U.S. Constitution. State law requires all 8th graders to pass a test on the Constitution before they can be promoted out of elementary school.

"They know they have to pass that test," says Nancy Banks, one of Goudy's two 8th-grade teachers. "It gives us a little magic from January to June."

The test is often administered more than once.

"When I was principal at Schubert [elementary], we had to give the test to some kids five times so the sixth time they would know what it meant," explained Thomas J. McDonald, who for 20 years has been Goudy's principal.

"That was a better school," said McDonald, "so we certainly have to do that here."

At Goudy, one of the public school system's 402 regular elementary schools, everybody knows the unwritten policy:

Eighth-graders do not flunk.

By the time the children walk into Goudy's 8th-grade classrooms, they have been in school for 8 and sometimes even 9 or 10 years.

In Room 304, Bernice Eiland teaches the brightest 8th graders. These children study from a history book where Ronald Reagan is president.

Next door, Room 302 is for the 8th graders who are farthest behind. Nancy Banks teaches a split class with these 8th graders mixed together with the highest-ranking 7th graders. Her students study history from a text that ends during the presidency of Richard M. Nixon.

Enter Room 304:

Eiland is trying to explain a worksheet on word meanings. She stops to reprimand Margarita Rodriguez for tossing a gum wrapper toward the waste basket. She remarks on the diet of a boy who is making smacking noises as he sucks on a piece of candy before 10 a.m. Then she continues on, explaining each and every direction on the worksheet before she will allow the students to begin.

"What are you supposed to write on your paper first?" she begins.

"Following directions is the most important thing in the world. Life is direction."

She is interrupted by a ripping sound.

"James, that is not the way to turn your page. To turn it over you take the top of the page not the bottom. Demetris, put your book on your desk. Tillis, is that your nice coat on the floor?

"Lastly," Eiland continues, "we have drawing conclusions. What does it mean to draw conclusions? James?"

No answer.

"Mark?"

"Drawing the end?"

"Get out your dictionaries," Eiland commands, sighing. The students all reach into their desks. "Find the word 'conclusion' and read what it means."

Enter Room 302:

The math assignment is on long division. Decimals are involved. Chanel Branch is hiding her pink calculator under her desk to do the problems. The children are chewing gum. Talking. Banks has done her best to give individual attention to everyone who needs it but this exercise dissolves into chaos when the students become frustrated by their inability to do the work.

"Shh! Shh!" begs Banks. She is clapping her hands for emphasis and her voice is getting strained.

"Boys and girls, *please*. Shernette, listen. Wanda, listen. You can learn from your mistakes as much as anything else."

From these classrooms emerge the children the public schools have groomed to become high school freshmen in the fall.

Both Banks and Eiland say they often have to wonder what the teachers have been teaching during all the years of elementary school.

"Last year, I said to my kids, 'How many of you have studied the Civil War?' and they just looked at me," recalled Banks, a teacher for 33 years.

Eiland, who has taught for 18 years, has made similar discoveries.

"Some of these children know nothing about government," she said. "We were having a lesson about the Amendments one day and I asked the children what it meant to bear arms. One of them said like two arms put through a shirt.

"Many of these kids have been lost during grammar school," said Eiland. "When they get to 8th grade, the job is to get them back."

'When I go out the door in the morning," said 8th grader Chanel Branch, "my little boy be holding onto my leg, crying sometimes. When I get home after school, he be asleep. He misses me when I be at school, and I miss him, too."

Chanel, who became pregnant when she was 12, is a short girl still plump from weight gained during pregnancy. She works hard to keep up with her studies but says it is difficult to do all of her homework at the same time she is trying to care for her son. She named her baby Stephen Dwayne after the doctor who delivered him.

The Tribune asked members of Goudy's Class of 1988 to write essays entitled, "Where do I go from here?" about their plans after graduation.

In hers, Chanel said she wants to graduate from high school and become a "post lady" who delivers mail.

"I could support my baby and help him get a good education and send him through college," Chanel wrote. "If he have kids he will know how to support them and not run out on them like most guys do."

Kim Le was the only student to aspire to the medical profession. He wants to study to be a doctor.

"When I became a very well doctor," Kim wrote, "I would traveled to every poor country to help the people there got well."

Robert Crawford is a 13-year-old who flunked last year. He was making Bs and Cs in his second year of 7th grade when, over the protests of his classroom teacher, he was promoted into 8th grade because the school counselor said he was doing well in reading and his standardized test scores suggested that he was capable of more challenging work.

After he graduates from college with a business major, Crawford said, he plans to open an office in California or Hawaii and own a "lakefront beach home."

"And i'm going to be driving my ninety thousand dollar ferrari. Then by day i'm going to be a lawyer by day and a peaceful man by night," Robert wrote.

James Traywick's plans include getting a scholarship to attend college and getting a job as a bank clerk during his second year as a business major.

"I will get a job at IBM as a data processer," he wrote. "After my second year I will get a loan for a fiero . . . Then after I find me a girlfriend I will propos to her. we will get marry on June third. After we get marry I will by a plane trip to Rio. After we get back from Rio I'll start saving money to by a swimg pool."

Roy Nunez plans to attend a junior college after high school graduation so he will be better prepared for college.

"When I get to college I plan on taking engineering classes and play sports," he wrote. "I want to play for a baseball team and if baseball doesnt work out, Ill have my education to fall back on."

Raul Martinez wants to study technical training in high school.

"When and if I graduate High school I want to go to college and get enginerir training," Raul wrote. "if I graduate college I want to Learn How to fix cars and trucks and drive them. But I don't want to drive those Little pizza trucks, I want to drive the "Big rigs" the 18 wheelers Like my father."

After spending two years in classrooms for children with behavior problems, William Tillis was "mainstreamed" into Bernice Eiland's regular classroom this year to prepare for his entry into high school. He has been doing well.

"A lot of times, being in that room made me feel down, like I wasn't no good," explained William, a slender boy who said he often baby-sits his six younger brothers and sisters.

In his essay, he wrote: "When I get in my freshman year, I am going to play basketball, or football. . . . I hope to go to a good college and when I get to colleg I will do six years and get a good degree."

Margarita Rodriguez, a shy girl with a pretty smile, wrote that she plans to attend "Amusen" high school and after that, go to college for four years.

"After I finish College," she wrote, "I want to work with Computers or be an actress."

Candy Gutshall says her mother talks often with her about the importance of staying in school. Her mother, Debbie, said she ditched a lot of classes while at

Goudy. She graduated from 8th grade, but dropped out of high school in her freshman year.

"After my 4 years of high school," wrote Candy, "I want to try to find a small job. Then I hope to get a better job later in life. I want to try and get a job as a secretary." Candy also mentioned that she hopes to find a "good-looking guy with money" to marry and who will take her on a week-long honeymoon in Hawaii.

One morning this year, three Chicago police squad cars sped to Goudy after Ronald Sims' teacher told the principal she thought that he was hiding a weapon in his desk. The police, according to Principal McDonald, found a real knife and a toy gun stashed among Ronald's school books.

In his essay, Ronald wrote about the challenge of staying in high school.

"When I do get to High School," he wrote, "I going to try my best to stay in school and not be on the streets . . . High school is going to be tuff, but I'm going to bare with it."

Detric Butler, who says he wants to pursue a career in either decorating, electrical work or machine trades, said that in whatever he does, he wants to be someone who does a good job and offers young children hope.

"The best that I can do for my self and the future of this world is to be a great role model such as Martin Luther King, Daniel Hale to the young people of the future."

Goudy has no organized sports, so Marc Venton plays on Chicago Park District teams. He plans to attend college on a football scholarship and would take courses in accounting because he would need something "to fall back on" if sports did not work out.

"After all my years of playing football I'll be recognized as a great player and drafted into professional football," Venton wrote. He said he would buy his mother a house with his earnings, travel the world when age forces him to retire, and then live off the income he will make from the four apartment buildings he will own.

Hector Ayala intends to graduate with honors from "Lame Technical" high school and hopes to play on the football team there. He said he would also take courses in math and science to prepare for college.

"After, college If I an mot drafted by a proffesional football team, I would go farther in my career and become a lawyer," Hector wrote.

"If I an prosperous in a business or become a succesful Lawyer, I would like to get married, buy a house, near a stream or river, have a car, and start a family. I would also like to give money to charities and special association to help the meedy.

"Finally, I'll retire and live the rest of my days with my family. I chose a river to be by my house because I would also like to go fishing three times a week after I retire."

Nearly all of Goudy's prospective graduates were assembled in Room 304 one afternoon to hear a counselor from Senn Metropolitan High School make her pitch. "Don't overlook your neighborhood high school" was the topic.

Though members of the Class of 1988 applied to eight different public high schools, most of those who stay in the

Uptown neighborhood and go on to high school will either by choice or by default become members of the freshman class at Senn, 5900 N. Glenwood Ave.

The counselor stood at the back of the room and clicked slides through the projector while speaking with the rehearsed enthusiasm of an airline stewardess explaining how to locate the emergency exit doors.

"Honors level means the work is a little bit harder," she offered. Ronald Sims, who was lying across a desktop, looked at classmate Detric Butler and rolled his eyes.

When the counselor flashed a vintage photograph of Senn's first faculty from 75 years ago, Sharese Scott put her head down on a desk. When she looked up once the presentation was through, the girl had sleepy eyes.

To a group of children for whom public school has meant little more than the bare essentials of reading, spelling, math, a little history and a lot of repetitive remedial exercises, this counselor talked about "program options" available in a school with a staff as big as three of Goudy's 1988 graduating classes combined.

"Wow!" Demetris Smith exclaimed in a loud whisper when she said that Senn offers art classes and that a student there designed the city's vehicle sticker one year.

The colors will be gold and burgundy. They will wear caps and gowns.

Teachers have grown accustomed to the wrinkles. Most years, only a fraction of the class follows directions properly so that the folds in the gowns that come

from shipment relax out.

It will cost nearly $30 for each child to take part in 8th-grade graduation this year. It must be paid in cash. School counselor Barbara Boxton said she ordered the "deluxe package" and among the things the money will buy are the class portraits, autograph books, ribbons, caps and gowns, the diploma cover and the special graduation lunch.

Most families will invest even more in clothes.

"They go all out," explained Boxton, who said that some parents buy their daughters formal dresses for graduation that look like lacey bridal gowns.

Last year, the boy at the bottom of the graduating class was dressed better than anyone else.

"He attended only one class during the school day, and that was to learn how to read," recalled teacher Fani Cahill. "And he showed up for graduation in a white tuxedo with a pink cummerbund."

The school usually ends up spending about $300 on each graduation, said Boxton, to cover expenses including the entire graduation package for children whose families cannot afford to pay.

Though he does not like to admit to it, Principal McDonald can be a soft-touch at graduation time. He has been known to dip into his pocket and pay for a new dress or two so a classmate can look just as special as a friend.

June 28 will be a milestone for the 8th-grade students who are a part of the Class of 1988 at Goudy Elementary School.

For if present trends continue within Chicago Public Schools, it will be the only graduation that about half of these children will ever have.

Measuring Up: *Goudy Elementary School 8th graders are measured for their burgundy-and-gold caps and gowns as their graduation approaches.*

How the promise turned out for 10

*'We should have been
studying in 5th grade.'*

As graduation for the high school Class of 1988 nears, what has become of the children who entered 1st grade in Chicago Public Schools 12 years ago?

The year was 1976, a time marking the United States bicentennial, when Americans hailed the nation's entry into a third century of promise.

That fall, 39,000 six-year-olds packed up their pencils and marched off to the city's schools in search of that promise. Among them were more than 100 children entering 1st grade at Goudy Elementary School, 5120 N. Winthrop Ave.

Where are the 1st graders now? What do they think of their years spent in the Chicago public schools? To find out, The Tribune tracked down 10 former Goudy students.

Of the 10, five now attend Chicago high schools and plan to graduate with the Class of 1988. One attends school in suburban Streamwood and expects to graduate next year. Four have dropped out of Chicago public high schools.

Three of the dropouts later enrolled in alternative schools. One is married and has a child. One recently completed a prison term for strong-arm robbery.

Interviews revealed that few of them felt the effect of dramatic changes in the school system over the 12 years.

None were aware teachers had changed the way they taught reading. Few realized schools had switched to a "graded" system of instruction from a "nongraded" or "continuous progress" system in which a child moves at his or her own pace.

Few knew the school system went broke in 1979. None knew the faculty had been integrated or that the school board had attempted to desegregate the schools.

Most didn't know about magnet schools. Most never considered going to anything but a public school.

All were unaware that the Chicago schools have had four general superintendents since 1976. And while all could identify Ruth Love as one of the superintendents, only one recognized the name of Manford Byrd Jr., the current superintendent.

The opinions expressed below were excerpted and condensed from lengthy interviews with 10 of the former Goudy 1st graders:

Alice Louie, 18

Lane Technical High, Class of 1988
  Attended Goudy and Peirce elementary schools and
Lane.

I'm pretty satisfied with my education. Chicago schools are pretty competitive because the students come from a variety of backgrounds.

I chose Lane over Senn because I felt Lane would be more academically challenging.

My parents motivated me. They said it was important for me to stay in school. Of course, I wanted to stay in myself. I was always a good student. I also chose friends like myself.

I learned to read in school, and on my own. My parents couldn't help me in English. I just picked it up, with no special help.

We got special math books at Goudy, so we could progress. I liked it better than using the regular books. School was more interesting. It wasn't so boring as when you already know the material.

What bothered me about teacher strikes, I had to stay a month later in the summer. But I got the same education. There were strikes both years I was to graduate. This year, colleges still wanted transcripts and applications on time, but because of the strike the school counselors had to rush the ap-

College-bound: *"I've been accepted at De Paul University and the University of Illinois at Chicago," says Alice Louie.*

plications for us in a limited amount of time.

I've planned a career in accounting. I've been accepted at De Paul University and the University of Illinois at Chicago.

Toni Vermillion, 17

Dropped out in 1985
   Attended Goudy, Swift, Haugen elementary schools, Arai middle school, an Indian reservation school, Senn and Truman Alternative High School. Paroled from a juvenile detention center March 3, 1988 after serving eight months for strong-arm robbery.

Wrong crowd: "I was . . . hanging out, smoking pot. I didn't want to go to high school. I got into the wrong crowd," says Toni Vermillion.

I wouldn't do anything to change the schools, except maybe give the teachers fewer students. I didn't learn because there were so many students. I figure they should have tutors like I do now.

I like the school here (Illinois Youth Center). I love it. This place is helping me know what's going on. Now, I'm more interested. I learn much more. They spend more time with me. They are willing to go over things with me. They are more patient than my teachers in 4th or 5th grade.

In 4th grade, they were switching me around. At Goudy, I was tested after school got too easy and got put in another class. I didn't want to go. I didn't like being switched . . . I was too scared about the kids. I finally got used to it.

The teachers used to tell me they were too busy to help. I missed a lot of things. In 8th grade, when I graduated, I didn't know my times (multiplication) tables.

I never liked grade school. Being a shy person, I wanted to be . . . at home.

I remember my mother would stay home (from work) sometimes and teach us. She taught us how to divide. She got us to read. She didn't want us sitting in front of TV.

After grade school, I was doing my own thing. Hanging out, smoking pot. I didn't want to go to high school. I got into the wrong crowd. That's what happened. Typical drug-users.

I didn't want to go to any high school in Chicago. I was afraid of getting into trouble.

My mom told us we could go anywhere, so I picked the American Indian Boarding School in South Dakota.

Looking back, I'd try to apply myself. I'd try to learn more. I don't know nothing right now.

I plan to go back to Truman, where I have a tutor. I plan to go to college after I get my G.E.D. Hopefully, I'd like to become a counselor. I want to help kids like me, kids that will be in my shoes.

I hope to live in the country. Or the suburbs, not Chicago. I don't expect to be married. Children? Maybe. If I had to live in Chicago, I'd send them to private schools. I think they're better. I didn't learn too much in public school.

Manuel Rodriguez, 17

Dropped out in 1986
  Attended Goudy and Nobel elementary schools and
Senn and Roosevelt high schools.

Chicago schools? They were good schools. I left because I just don't like school. I don't like nothing about it. I don't like getting up early to go to school.

In 8th grade, I was in this class where they help you when you're slow. I liked that. I was, like, the only one in the class. I had trouble with math. It helped me graduate.

My sophomore year, I started drinking and getting high, and I lost interest in school. I went into drug rehab.

My wife dropped out, too. Now she goes to an alternative high school—Prologue. She's in her last year.

My son, he was born last November. I'd send him to Chicago schools. I'd like him to finish high school.

If I was to start over again, I'd try harder. When I was growing up, I was in gangs. I wouldn't do it again. Why? I don't know.

I was working at a paint-thinner factory nine months. I got laid off. I really quit, because I couldn't get along with some of the people. We're living on welfare. Unemployment insurance? I don't know about unemployment insurance.

I'm not disappointed I didn't get my diploma. You don't need a high school diploma.

I might go to trade school and be a mechanic. You don't need a diploma to take a trade. If you don't need one, why do it?"

No need: "You don't need a diploma to take a trade. If you don't need one, why do it?," says Manuel Rodriguez, with his wife and child looking on.

Dawn Dodge, 17

Senn Metropolitan High, Class of 1988
Attended only Goudy and Senn.

Sometimes you just want to give up. It's just too much to take.

It's the teachers. Sometimes they don't care. Or they don't explain the work. I have a teacher, she don't explain it, so I think, 'Why should I do it?'

Literature is my favorite subject. Math is my worst.

This school feels like prison. You can't leave. We used to go out for lunch.

My mother helped me get where I am. My teachers at Goudy and Senn also helped.

Teacher strikes get on my nerves. . . . They strike for money, but I never see improvement . . . All I see is fancier cars.

I'll be a famous actress of stage, screen—everything. I love acting. It's a life-long ambition. That's the way I keep out of trouble. I act my way out of it.

Odalis Roldan, 18

Senn Metropolitan High, Class of 1988
Attended only Goudy and Senn.

My mother didn't want me to come here (Senn), but she let me give it a try. She was afraid of me getting into gangs, fights, drugs and all that. It was good advice.

She wanted to send me to St. Scholastica, but I didn't want to go to an all-girls school. I wanted a mix.

During my last two years, my parents have pushed me, especially my dad. They said if I wanted to make something of myself, I'd have to study.

Look at the teachers. In Chicago schools, some teachers just don't care, particularly if the kids aren't paying attention.

In grammar school, reading was confusing. Each teacher taught her own way. When students complained that their other teacher taught another way, the teacher said, 'She's wrong.'

I hope to be a pediatrician, a pharmacist or a law enforcement official. I've applied to the University of Illinois at Chicago and Northeastern Illinois University.

Stacey Peterson, 18

Senn Metropolitan High, Class of 1988
Attended Goudy, Disney Magnet, an elementary school in Florida and Senn.

I went back to Goudy about three months ago. I couldn't believe how much they have improved the school— with computers. Those kids just type, type, type away with headphones.

I like Senn. The teachers are nice. The classes—well, you can get a bunch of wildcats—but all my classes this year are pretty neat. If I had to change over Senn, I don't think there's anything I'd change. As the years progress, it gets better and better. They really make you work. My only trouble is math. I've always had trouble with that.

When I was tested for reading at Disney, I was terrible. They put me in a group of eight or nine kids. It helped me a lot. By the time I entered high school, I tested between the 7th and 8th grade.

By the year 2000, I hope to be well into a military career. I want to join the Army. . . . I've taken a test for the Air Force, but I like the Army's commercials better.

Joselyn Donis, 17
Senn Metropolitan High, Class of 1988
Attended only Goudy and Senn

I like school. The students I hang around with like school, too. The only problem I've had, up to now, is with English. I don't like English at all. I've always had a hard time. The classes I'm put into, the teachers end up giving harder stuff.

My English teacher gives us the book and questions that I can't understand. Like, 'What do you think the author was trying to tell you?' I can't understand her. Lots of students have the same opinion.

My parents have always been strict about my grades. My mother and dad are always telling us, 'Do your homework. Let me know. I'll help if you have problems.'

Right now, I feel I haven't tried as much as I should. I guess, because, when you get to your senior year, you have so many decisions.

In another 12 years, I hope to be working, finished with college maybe married, and probably have children. Hopefully by that time, schools will be improved.

Senn Students: *Four students who started at Goudy look to the future and reflect on the past. Clockwise from top left: Stacey Peterson, Joselyn Donis, Odalis Roldan and Dawn Dodge.*

Terri Turney, 17
Tammi Turney, 17
Prologue Alternative High, Class of 1989
  Attended Goudy, various Indian reservation
schools, Senn Indian branch and Prologue.

Terri dropped out a few weeks after entering Senn:

At Senn, they just handed me a math paper and told me to do it. I asked for help, but the teacher said I should ask the person next to me. I needed a teacher to sit down and explain it.

My counselor said if I needed help to come to her. She was my English teacher. It helped a little bit, but I still didn't understand math.

I hung around with a crowd. Just girls. No boys. They were jerks, most of the boys I knew. Most of the girls in my crowd dropped out the same time. After a couple of months, I realized I needed school. I couldn't get a job.

Held back: *"We got held back in 5th grade. Most of us did. The teacher just held parties," says Tammi Turney (right), with her twin, Terri.*

I wanted to go to Amundsen, but when my teacher asked for hands, I goofed that one up. She put down I didn't want to go there. I didn't understand her question because I'd been talking.

Tammi left Senn three months later:

When Terri dropped out, that left me alone. There was a lot of gang trouble for me. Some people I hung around with were into gangs, so other gang members started pestering me. When I said I didn't belong, they tried to get me to join.

I told my counselor, and she made me point out the kids. It got worse. They didn't listen to the lady.

I took a little longer to drop out. I only showed up for certain classes. They signed me up for biology, and they started cutting up things. When they started cutting up pigs, that was it. I couldn't handle that.

There also were drugs going through the school. Senn was just too big. The teachers and guards couldn't handle it all. Here at Prologue, gang members have to sign a contract that there won't be any gang recruitment. And no fighting.

I didn't think I needed to finish school. But after I got here, I decided to stay. My scores went up. I thought if I got a diploma, everybody would leave me alone.

We got held back in 5th grade. Most of us did. The teacher just held parties. She'd look around and ask, 'Who's birthday is it?'

Terri: We was at the park all the time.

Tammi: They made us pay for certain books in 5th grade. I remember I had to pay for my workbook, but my mother had an operation, so we had to go to my stepfather to pay.

Some kids didn't have the money. The teacher would give us homework out of the book. They couldn't do it. It took me a week and a half before I could pay. It caused a lot of problems with class work.

All the kids we knew who went to Senn didn't stay. Those who made it left Goudy or weren't in 5th grade with us. One held back with us in 5th graduated after 7th grade.

Terri: I wasn't ready to graduate. I needed to learn more. We should have been studying in 5th grade instead of messing around. In 7th and 8th grade, the teacher kept trying to explain that school was important.

Tammi: But they never told us what education was, why you needed it. We were just told to do it. If we began over, we'd study harder. A lot harder. If they had explained the importance of education, a lot of kids would have stuck it out.

Our mother was too busy to sit down and explain it to us. I don't blame my mother. There were five of us. She had too much to handle. She just worked.

Terri: I want to go to DeVry or American Business Institute. I hope to be a computer programmer. I ain't getting married, but I like kids. I'd send my kids to private school, not public. I want to make it safe.

Tammi: The teachers here say college is great. I'm interested in a law career. I want to go to an expensive college. I don't want to get married.

Terri: You can't get nowhere without education.

Inalvis Fiallo, 18

Streamwood High School, Class of 1989
    Attended Goudy, Peirce, and elementary schools in Florida; St. Scholastica, Hialeah (Fla.) and Streamwood high schools.

My family didn't want me to go to a Chicago high school. They wanted me to go to a private school. I had no choice. They didn't want me to go to Senn because of the gangs. They were concerned for my safety.

I wanted to go to Amundsen, but it had the same problem. So I went to St. Scholastica. At first, I didn't think I'd like Catholic school. I didn't know anybody. But I liked it. Then I moved to Florida.

I didn't like high school there because most of the classes were taught in Spanish, and they confused me. So, I moved back to the Chicago area to live with my aunt.

I disagree with those who say Chicago has a poor school system. It depends if the student wants to learn or not. They don't take their education seriously.

My family has encouraged me to prepare for a career.

When I went to Goudy, it wasn't that bad. . . . There was one teacher at Peirce, a math teacher. He was into education, a positive influence. He kept telling us we won't get anywhere without education.

I wanted to be a 1st grade teacher when I was in 6th grade. Now, I hope to become a flight attendant.

If I were to do it over, I wouldn't change a thing. I wouldn't mind sending my children to Chicago schools.

Illustration by Tom Herzberg

Forging new schools: Innovations pay off elsewhere

'Every child can learn; it's up to us to find the way'

Chicago lags far behind the growing national effort to find ways to educate the impoverished children of big cities.

No one place has the entire solution. Little pieces of the urban education puzzle are being filled in here and there.

Chicago has some pieces, but fewer than other cities. In fact, the school bureaucracy and the teachers union here have even stymied ideas that have worked elsewhere.

One of the most promising experiments in Chicago is one that is trying to give intense help, beginning even before birth, to all the children who will enter kindergarten at Beethoven Elementary School from 1992 to 1994.

The Beethoven Project, however, was created by people totally outside the school system and is funded by private foundation grants and state and federal money.

It was the only Chicago program highlighted at a national meeting in Washington in December on the challenge of educating poor and minority children.

As part of a seven-month examination of the Chicago schools, Tribune reporters looked at innovative school and community programs throughout the country. Some of them are longstanding, with proven track records. Others are new and untested, but promising. All have something important to say about what needs to be done to fix the Chicago schools.

In Rochester, N.Y., Supt. Peter McWalters and teachers union president Adam Urbanski may be two of the most unlikely school leaders in America.

McWalters is a former Peace Corps volunteer with degrees in Oriental history, philosophy and theology. Urbanski is a Polish immigrant with a doctorate in American social history.

Together, the two men have set aside the traditional negotiating methods—methods that have given Chicago nine teachers strikes in 19 years and a contract that makes the union the most powerful force in the school system—to arrive at a contract that could serve as a model for school districts around the nation.

The cornerstone of their agreement is that the children come first.

"For years we have had a system of education which has not served poor, urban, minority children," McWalters said. "That system has an incredible ability to perpetuate itself. It is quite capable of chewing up any reforms thrown at it and emerging when the dust settles quite like it was before.

"To break it, I have to hit it with so many impulses that it goes into complete overload and breaks down totally. Only then can we start to rebuild it into something that works for poor children."

McWalters and Urbanski went one-on-one to negotiate a contract that will gradually replace seniority with skill as the major criterion for teacher assignment in the 33,000-student district. The contract also includes an innovative process through which the union works with the board to get rid of incompetent teachers.

The contract sets in motion a system for giving each school a committee of parents, teachers and administrators to select new teachers based on ability.

"There was anxiety that departs from traditional unionism," Urbanski said. "But I have no problem in changing rules that were written for another time."

A career ladder replaces the typical salary schedule. Teacher salaries will reach an average of $45,000 in five years, and lead teachers—those who work a longer school year, take on extra duties and waive seniority rights in assignment to schools—will be able to earn as much as $70,000 a year.

"The new contract says you get more money and prestige if you work longer and have more responsibility—just like the real world," Urbanski said.

McWalters wanted teachers to be accountable for student performance— but not in the sense that one teacher would be responsible only for his or her class. He wanted all teachers in the school to take responsibility for the learning in the entire school.

"And I said we would do that," Urbanski said. "But only if teachers were paid enough and were allowed into the decision-making process. It's not that we'll work harder only if you pay us more, but that we need to attract people who are smart enough to do these new things."

Rochester's plan for dealing with incompetent teachers, still relatively untested, appears to be an improvement over Chicago's. In Rochester, the mentor teacher assigned to work with a failing teacher can stop at any time within two semesters if a panel of 4 teachers and 3 administrators decide that no further help is needed or would be productive. In Illinois, under state law, the consultation must be for a two full semesters.

If the Rochester panel decides that the teacher has improved enough to be considered competent, he or she remains. If not, the panel recommends that the superintendent ask the board to fire the teacher.

"We will admit that the intervention was unsuccessful," Urbanski said. "If no real learning is going on, that person should not be in the classroom." Rochester teachers say they will wait to see the impact of the changes, but they are excited about the possibilities.

"I've been here 18 years and I

thought I'd have to leave teaching for an administrative post to earn more money," said James Hagan, 5th-grade teacher at Clara Barton Elementary School. "But the career ladder opens up more opportunities."

Paula Hanson, who teaches learning-disabled children at Barton, says she hopes that the changes "will revolutionize education by letting those closest to the children, the teachers, make the key decisions."

McWalters wants the "revolution" to also change the way teachers perceive children, especially disadvantaged children.

Much of Rochester's middle class, like Chicago's, has fled to the suburbs, leaving the city schools with an enrollment that is mostly black and Hispanic and overwhelmingly poor. Four out of five children come to kindergarten already behind their peers nationwide.

"Every child that walks through that door has to be acceptable, as he is, not how you would like him to be," McWalters said. "We've got all these programs that sift kids, that sort them and try to get them out of our regular classrooms. We have to stop all that. Every child can learn and it is up to us to find the way he learns and teach him in that way.

"Teachers have to feel towards children: 'Your future is my future. I can only succeed if you succeed.' "

Six states have the power to take over school districts that become educationally bankrupt—so deficient in their ability to deliver an education or manage their resources that their students are not learning.

Recently, New Jersey became the first of those states to begin the legal process to seize control of a school district, the 29,000-student Jersey City Schools.

Both New Jersey and several of the other states who have such laws—Arkansas, Georgia, Kentucky, South Carolina and Texas—have used the threat of a takeover to spur districts to make improvements.

In announcing the first test of the five-month-old New Jersey law, Education Commissioner Saul Cooperman said the Jersey City schools were plagued by "a cycle of failure," and that the district had "reached a state of managerial bankruptcy."

Cooperman cited "political patronage, union pressure and cronyism . . . in the hiring, firing, promoting and deployment of staff" as a major part of the reason for the proposed takeover of the state's second largest school district.

If Cooperman wins an expected court challenge, he would have the power to fire the school superintendent and his assistant superintendents, to abolish the present school board and replace it with a new one, and to evaluate the principals in the district's 33 schools.

What happens will be watched throughout the nation to see if state takeovers can turn urban school districts around. Some experts believe that some kind of political upheaval of this magnitude will be needed to make moribund districts change.

Some in the Jersey City schools say they are weary of the internecine battles in the district and see the takeover as the only hope.

"Takeover is the only salvation for the system," John Phillips, president of the local principal's association, told the Wall Street Journal. "We're middle management and we're being squeezed from the top and the bottom. We have no real authority to run our schools."

Owen Bradford Butler, retired board chairman of Procter and Gamble, is a man one would expect to be more familiar with corporate bottom lines than with toddlers.

But when Butler spoke to a gathering of hundreds of educators at a national conference on poor and minority children in Washington in December, he had a surprisingly simple message.

"To improve education, society and our economy, the best single investment we could make is one year of high-quality preschool nurturing for every 3-year-old at-risk child," Butler said.

"Where parents can't or won't take care of their preschool children, we as a society must step in—in our own self-interest," he said. "You don't need a heart to take care of disadvantaged children. You just need a head."

Early childhood education is crucial in Chicago where many preschoolers have mothers who themselves are still teenagers.

But the Illinois General Assembly has reneged on its 1985 promise to fund early childhood programs, says State School Supt. Ted Sanders.

"Today, we can report absolutely no progress in meeting the commitment of 1985," Sanders said. "We wanted to have 112,000 children in early childhood education by now. The first year of the reform we had 5,000; the second year, 7,000; and now we have fallen back to 6,300.

"We get constant opposition from Downstate districts who don't want money earmarked for early childhood education," Sanders said. He said opposition also comes from conservative groups such as Phyllis Schlafly's Eagle Forum and conservative lawmakers such as State Rep. Penny Pullen (R., Park Ridge).

"This is the most politically volatile reform we've tried to accomplish, and we've literally made no gains," Sanders said.

Private groups have tried to pick up the slack, but there is only so much they can do with limited funds.

The Beethoven Project is a five-year program to make sure that the 300 or so children who will make up the kindergarten classes of 1992 through 1994 at Beethoven Elementary School, 25 W. 47th St., will be ready to learn.

The emphasis is on nurturing and educating both mothers and babies, and it starts before the babies are born. So far, 110 mothers or pregnant women are in the program, in which trained counselors provide comprehensive care to children who are born into six buildings of the Robert Taylor Homes public housing project.

The program is a joint effort between the Chicago Urban League and the Ounce of Prevention Fund. It was the brainchild of Irving S. Harris, a Chicago businessman and philanthropist who helped start the program.

Few programs are as intense as Beethoven, but other states have moved ahead of Illinois in providing early help to children.

Missouri has 108,000 families involved in a Parents as Teachers Program in which every parent with a 4-year-old can have someone come into their home to teach them how and what to teach their child.

Arkansas has 1,000 preschool children in 10 of its poorest school districts enrolled in Home Instruction Programs in which mothers are taught how to teach their toddlers. Gov. Bill Clinton said in December his goal was to expand the program to all 19,000 Arkansas children who would benefit from it.

"We need to break the intergenerational cycle of failure," Missouri Gov. John Ashcroft told the December meeting in Washington. "We need to train all parents to be their child's first and best teacher.

"The chances of success are getting slimmer in our society," Ashcroft said. "We kid ourselves when we say that we are a child-oriented society."

The Boston Compact, started in 1982, is an example of how corporate social responsibility can boost an ailing urban school district by giving the hope of employment to its students.

Boston, unlike Chicago, has a booming economy where jobs exceed workers qualified to fill them. But because the number of people entering the work force is decreasing, Chicago will soon be in the same predicament.

An alliance between the Boston School Committee and several Boston businesses, unions, colleges and universities, the compact gives Boston public school students preference over private or suburban school graduates in apprenticeships and jobs.

In return, the schools are trying to improve attendance, reading and math scores and the graduation rate.

About 3,000 students a year graduate from Boston public high schools. About 2,000 go to college or find jobs on their own. The remaining 1,000, mostly minorities, are the group the compact tries to serve.

"It's important to invest in the future work force," said Edward Dooley, executive director of the compact. "Boston's future depends on these children. Everyone will suffer if they don't have jobs."

But in highly educated Boston, where 44 percent of the clerical pool in 1985 had college degrees, poor students, often high school dropouts, are at a definite disadvantage. The compact tries to even their odds.

"Part of the barrier is a class bias and a race bias," Dooley said. "We are an advocate for the lower class. We are their 'old-boy network.' "

The compact has gotten jobs for more than 2,000 students in five years. Several Boston area colleges and universities have pledged to increase by 25 percent their acceptance of public school graduates. Boston trade unions have agreed to increase opportunities in apprenticeship programs.

The schools have had a tougher time

holding up their end of the compact. A staggering number of Boston students continue to drop out of school and have math and reading scores below grade level.

But Al Holland, principal of Jeremiah Burke High School in Boston's Roxbury neighborhood, said benefits are already being seen.

"The program has made all the difference in the world for students," Holland said. "It has given them a reason to hope, a future."

In Chicago, such a plan was scuttled in November when, after months of negotiations with the Chicago Partnership for Educational Progress, Supt. Manford Byrd Jr. refused to agree to improve the schools in exchange for jobs, demanded six times as many jobs per year as business leaders thought they could provide, and demanded help from business in getting more state money.

Byrd said he turned down the plan because he did not think it was fair to tie jobs to student performance.

E very day dozens of parents sit in classrooms, monitor washrooms and police halls at Washington Preparatory High School in Los Angeles, in a black and Hispanic neighborhood six miles west of Watts and across the street from the site of a recent street gang killing.

The parents are there on Saturdays to take parenting classes. They are there in the evening when the parent-community council meets.

These are the kind of mothers and grandmothers that many people in Chicago say don't care enough to help run their schools, yet Principal George McKenna credits them with turning Washington Prep from a place that middle-class blacks fled to one with a 300-name waiting list for its magnet program.

"You need to give the parents real responsibility," McKenna said. "The teachers here know that there is a community that cares what goes on in the schools, they have to be accountable to these parents."

McKenna started with two interested parents from each homeroom and formed a core group that has reached out to other parents. Depending on what they do for the school, some get paid with federal antipoverty funds.

"It is a full-time job to get parents in the school—to get their friends and neighbors and fellow churchgoers in here—so I pay people to do it," McKenna said.

James P. Comer of the Yale Child Study Center has spent 20 years devising ways to get parents involved and have schools look after the social needs of poor children.

Comer and his four brothers and sisters have, between them, 13 college degrees. He says they owe that success to the casual conversations that took place almost weekly between his parents and teachers in the 1940s.

In 1968, Comer started to re-create those connections in two all-black, poverty-level New Haven, Conn., grade schools that ranked 32d and 33d in reading scores among 33 district schools.

Twenty years later, one of those

schools, and another he substituted when the first one closed, are ranked 3d and 4th in reading among 26 current New Haven grade schools. The schools have remained all-black and primarily poor.

Comer created positive situations to lure parents into the schools—pot luck suppers, fashion shows, academic fairs. Many of those parents, he said, remembered schools as threatening places filled with failure.

He also established what he calls a mental health team to talk about children's social and home problems.

At Robinson Middle School, for example, the team discovered that a disruptive child was reacting to his mother's drug addiction. The team found counseling for the mother and talked to the state's department of youth services about placing the boy in a foster home.

New Haven's positive experience is a stark contrast to Chicago's, where social workers and truant officers were cut this year to free up money for salary increases and where teachers say children have overwhelming problems that prevent them from learning.

Teachers, like others in high-stress jobs, need to be renewed to be able to continue their work.

But in Chicago, they get little more than mind-numbing "in-service training." College courses must be taken on their own time and paid for out of their own pocket.

Chicago teachers seldom have a chance to share ideas or learn to work together. That isolation makes change difficult.

Pittsburgh has a better idea.

The first major public school system in the nation to require every teacher to be retrained, Pittsburgh has instituted an eight-week program of renewal and revitalization.

Over the last five years, 840 teachers have gone through the program, at a cost of $11 million from foundation grants and school board funds.

Pittsburgh teachers say the renewal program has ignited a new love for teaching, produced valuable lessons on teaching techniques and created a new spirit among their ranks.

"First you turn the teachers around, then you turn the students around," said teacher Dolores Kubiak.

Before teachers can teach, they have to be in the classroom. Chicago cannot even consistently get its faculty to work, or find substitutes to fill in for all the absent teachers.

Los Angeles, a sprawling school system one-and-a-half times the size of Chicago's, has solved that problem through higher pay and stricter rules for substitutes. It needs fewer substitutes partly because its teachers are less likely to call in sick than Chicago teachers, but also because substitutes work more often, are paid more and get incentive pay for teaching in hard-to-staff schools.

Los Angeles had half the average number of unstaffed positions a day during the first semester compared to Chicago, despite its larger size.

Los Angeles substitutes who refuse more than 10 assignments each semester are bumped to the bottom of the availability list. Chicago substitutes can refuse any assignment.

"We don't allow subs to continually refuse assignments just because they don't want to work in certain schools," said Michael Boardie, director of the Los Angeles substitute center. "If we allowed subs to do that, we would have all kinds of problems."

The Chicago bureaucracy is preoccupied with changing numbers, but cares little about changing reality. This attitude filters down to teachers and students.

An overemphasis on reading and math scores on the Iowa Test of Basic Skills, combined with tight finances and priorities skewed to benefit bureaucrats, has pushed science, art, music and literature out of many classrooms, especially in low-achieving neighborhood schools.

It creates a situation where children talk about their "Iowas" but can't name the last book they read, and where Goudy Elementary School teacher Ruby Smith says her federally funded job with her low-achieving children is "to raise their scores."

Children who have the weakest skills in abstract thought, those who need to learn in concrete or subtle ways, are instead marched through endless exercises to train them how to answer multiple choice tests.

"The grade schools spend so much time on reading and math that by the time the students come to us, science is completely foreign to them," said Nancy Lewis, English department chairwoman at Manley High School, 2935 W. Polk St.

In New York City, one school has deliberately given up its coveted first place in the district in reading scores to spend more time on teaching.

"We were first in the district for four out of the past six years," said Principal Herbert Ross of P.S. 41, an elementary school located in one of the poorest areas of Brooklyn with an enrollment that is 87 percent black and 13 percent Hispanic.

"We were gearing the whole school to those tests—giving workshops, writing manuals," Ross said. "But then we looked at what we were doing. We were shortchanging the kids of their education. We backed off.

"We aren't No. 1 anymore, but we can live with ourselves."

No Teacher: *A Du Sable student waits in vain for a teacher. "We should require teachers and principals to take a sincerity oath," Mayor Sawyer says.*

Active parents are key to many reform programs

Educators, leaders offer blueprints for improvement

You suddenly find yourself with the power to change the Chicago Public Schools. What would you do?

This question was put to about 50 people with the power to make a difference. Three major themes emerge from their answers: The school system must reach out to involve parents, must improve teacher quality and must focus authority and responsibility on individual schools and principals.

Some of those whose comments were invited, including School Board President Frank Gardner, declined to respond for various reasons. What some who did respond had to say, edited and condensed to meet space constraints, appears in alphabetical order:

Michael Bakalis, dean, School of Education, Loyola University of Chicago:

Put the needs of children first. They now are secondary to the agendas of the union leadership, school board and political establishment.

Restructure the Chicago public schools bureaucracy, a system void of two essential ingredients—account-ability and creativity.

Eliminate the elitism and arrogance that now characterizes the system, one fearful of citizen involvement that often assumes the children can't learn.

Look at the lessons of schools in the system that work and at examples of parochial schools in the city that show substantial success, without the accompanying costly and inefficient bureaucracy.

Recognize that no single reform plan will totally solve Chicago's school problems, until the support systems of community and family are rebuilt.

Rather than becoming aloof from school issues, recognize that the political and business leadership must be intimately involved. The city's economic future is directly related to the viability of the school system.

Rev. Willie Barrow, national executive director, Operation PUSH:

Teachers should develop individual work plans for students. The plans should be written, taking into account the student's strengths and weaknesses, and should include realistic academic and behavioral goals. Students and teachers would sign off on the plans. Each should monitor student progress weekly.

The classroom student-teacher ratio should be no greater than 20 to 1.

Parent-teacher conferences should be scheduled for mid-semester to discuss student plans and academic progress and parental responsibility for monitoring home-community activities. Parents should be encouraged to take an interest in school through volunteer programs. Parent meetings should include discussion of standardized test scores.

A major community effort should be organized to get parents *en masse* to pick up report cards each grading period.

Educational curriculums should be flexible enough to accommodate differences in learning styles.

State Sen. Arthur Berman, chairman, Senate Elementary and Secondary Education Committee:

Reduce the Board of Education's central bureaucracy, coupled with a shift of personnel and funds to classrooms.

Negotiate performance-based contracts for principals on the basis of elements of student performance and achievement, parental involvement and safe learning environment.

Provide intensive teacher training, peer support and professional development. Increase the level of parent involvement in a strong advisory role to the school principal. Create a school educational authority to implement and achieve real reform and ensure that reforms are enacted in a predetermined, reasonable time frame.

Permit citywide participation in making nominations to the mayor for school board members.

Increase state funding closely tied to student and staff performance, and a cap on the board's administrative spending.

Chicago School Supt. Manford Byrd Jr.:

No citizen, be they parent, educator or resident, should be exempt or excluded from the responsibility for the well-being of the school system. There must be a national recommitment to public education, a broader understanding of its role in our democracy and a better appreciation for what it has done for development of our society.

As general superintendent of schools the past three years, I have exercised broad powers to improve the school system. Among these actions were a system-wide administrative reorganization which put more personnel in support of schools; the development and implementation of new comprehensive reading and mathematics programs in elementary schools; the development and implementation of new policies on homework and elementary school promotions; expanded preschool and kindergarten classes, an expanded summer school program and the restoration of after-school programs.

These and other key initiatives have been undertaken specifically to improve the academic performance of students, to provide them more and better opportunities for success and to address some of the particular needs of our atypical student population.

Gary A. Griffin, dean, College of Education, University of Illinois-Chicago:

A basic assumption about school success is that it is based upon people who have the wit and the will to engage in serious and systematic study and experimentation.

I believe the focus for change should be on the individual school. There must be a mutually reinforcing system of staff development and expectation-raising. Requisite knowledge must be distributed across the faculty, not lodged solely in the mind and heart of the principal.

For the redistribution of school leadership to have impact, teachers with leadership responsibilities must be recognized and rewarded. There must be recognition that teaching is primarily intellectual in nature. The clerical work teachers do must be reassigned.

School-based management, decentralization or whatever label is given the next wave of school reform cannot be brought off without ensuring that the necessary knowledge and skill is in place to make the school a reasonable place for decision-making.

Simply taking the keys from one unsuccessful group and giving them to another without the ability to develop successful schools won't wash. Current proposals for parent involvement, teacher decision-making, community

overseers and the like will continue to be politically attractive and intuitively appealing, but they are destined to be no more effective than business as usual.

Joseph Kellman, president, Globe Glass & Mirror Co.; founder, Better Boys Foundations:

Genuine realistic school reform should come about from a fully paid board of corporate executives.

I'm talking about "six-figure" executives—top educators and community people, with at least one labor person, working full-time. Salaries of such a corporate component would be supplemented by the corporate community.

This isn't a job for volunteers. We need experts to turn around a $2 billion corporation on the verge of bankruptcy.

Ada Lopez, member, Chicago Board of Education:

If we are to prepare our students for the year 2000, our curriculum must be re-examined, otherwise reform will only result in an exercise in social architecture. We also must re-examine our educational goals.

Our curriculum must emphasize development of logical and creative thinking, the ability to solve problems and communicate effectively, and development of a sense of civic responsibility.

Objectives related to these goals should be recognized and established as priority. Teaching too many short-term incidental factors, which quickly become irrelevant, should be replaced with more relevant factors, goals and objectives.

Richard M. Morrow, chairman of the board, Amoco Corp.:

Among the most pressing challenges are problems confronting disadvantaged children. These youngsters deserve special attention, particularly in the years before they enter the education process.

Quality preschool programs have been shown to be an effective means of encouraging disadvantaged young people to stay in school. Without early intervention, many will enter school lacking the social and intellectual experiences necessary for learning.

Schools must stress basic reading, writing and arithmetic education and the development of problem solving, communication and teamwork skills. Moreover, they must develop programs that encourage young people to stay in school.

Schools must create a learning environment where values are imparted, where concepts of right and wrong are stressed and where an appreciation for our democratic institutions is presented.

Patricia O'Hern, member, Chicago Board of Education:

Every citizen must face up to the responsibility that the child belongs to all of us. We must educate every child. We must support the child, including being a volunteer in school or making sure the child is prepared to learn when he gets there.

Responsibility also rests with the State of Illinois, which makes one of the lowest contributions to education in the nation. Real estate taxes in Chicago are not comparable to suburban districts. We need to face the reality of real estate taxes. We get what we pay for. We must raise the levy for education in Chicago.

The legislature must permit the system and administration to rid itself of teachers who are not functioning. We need a change in the state law. The current law leans toward the union. I'm not surprised: last year the union spent a half-million dollars in its lobbying efforts in Springfield.

Beyond that, you can't keep beating the system up. By doing so, you send a very negative message to our young people. We need to be more positive. All of us need to help, to get involved. It's just not money. We need to change some attitudes.

Eugene Sawyer, mayor of Chicago:

We need an all-out offensive to mobilize the entire Chicago metropolitan community in a " Don't Wait, Educate" campaign.

We should require teachers and principals to take a sincerity oath, pledging that "our youth can learn, our schools will teach."

We should convene a daylong meeting of the school board, teachers union and interested businesses to agree on a citywide, coordinated offensive to make getting an education fashionable. We should enlist celebrities to reinforce the pro-education message and saturate various media, public meetings and special events with this message.

We should cut at least 10 percent of the non-instructional fat from the central administration and redirect those funds to the classroom. We should wipe away rules that prohibit principals from being in charge of their schools. We should do away with marginally competent teachers.

To reinforce overall school management, we should put school superintendents on performance-based contracts, requiring them to achieve specific graduation and achievement test standards. Failure to achieve the goals should be considered a breach of contract and grounds for dismissal.

We should reward good teachers with higher salaries and institute a Chicago "Academy Awards" program for teachers, which not only would give them recognition but a cash award.

We should require parents, the most important players in school reform, to spend at least three hours a week working with their children on homework. Teachers should do report cards on parental involvement in their children's school work.

Loren Smith, CEO and chairman, Citicorp Savings of Illinois:

The main problem is one of management. We should borrow a solution from private industry—decentralization.

Put resources where the people are. Let priorities be set by the people who own the problem—the local parents, community, teachers and school principal. They own the problem and manage resources more efficiently.

James Thompson, governor of Illinois:

Chicago public schools can be improved by consistently offering quality education to all students. Selectively, the schools have shown this is possible.

This means sufficient early education programs for the youngest students and alternative education programs at the secondary level.

Another key to improvement is emphasis on prevention programs, so truants and dropouts can have their needs addressed before it's too late.

The school system must be accountable to the publics it serves. Staff and financial resources must be examined carefully and directed towards improved instruction. The schools must also be adequately funded with local and state resources so programs can be stable over time.

We should not be spending much time and energy on organization issues but focus on identifying the problems—high dropout rates, low student performance, lack of parental involvement, lack of trust by the business sector due to poor skills of graduates, inadequate and unstable funding—and resolving them together.

Jacqueline Vaughn, president, Chicago Teachers Union:

Chicago public schools can be improved through a restructured system that emphasizes a greater role for parents, shared decision-making between teachers, principals and parents on matters related to student performance, selection of textbooks and materials and expenditure of discretionary funds.

They can be improved by a significant reduction in administrative spending, with transfer of those savings to local schools where shared decision-making takes place on how to enhance the educational program to produce improved student achievement.

The present system could be improved by implementing the CTU model of school-based management at the local level and by enhancing the concept of shared decision-making between parents, teachers and principals.

Partnerships should be promoted between representatives of the school community, parents, teachers, principals and business and civic leaders to jointly seek new sources of revenue to finance educational improvements. Such improvements would include smaller class size, acquisition of textbooks and materials and the establishment or expansion of teacher training centers to retrain teachers in new technology and skills.

An editorial: How to rescue the worst schools in America

What will save Chicago's public schools, the worst in America?

Not the Chicago Board of Education. It hasn't the guts or know-how to make changes.

Not the superintendent of schools. Dr. Manford Byrd is shamefully ignorant about his own school system and has no idea how to improve it. His bloated bureaucracy soaks up school money and smothers efforts to change.

Not the teachers. The Chicago Teachers Union has a militant interest in only two things—getting more money for its members and preventing even the most incompetent of them from ever being fired.

Not Chicago's mayor. He doesn't count. Chicago mayors, past and present, have forfeited their role in school management and no longer have the political clout to make a difference.

Not the state legislature. Its leaders aren't concerned about Chicago schools, except when they are useful for political deal-making. Pending bills are hastily drafted and of dubious merit. No one wants to have to spend more tax dollars on a poor, black-majority system.

Not the governor. He's cozy with the unions and being squeezed everywhere for more tax dollars.

Not more money from the state government. Until drastic changes are

© 1988 CHICAGO TRIBUNE

made in the system, more tax dollars simply will be sopped up by the bureaucracy and by teachers' salaries without making a dime's worth of difference to children.

Not the report on school reform from the high-level Education Summit. Its 45 prestigious members wasted so much time and good will trying to reach a consensus without treading on vested interests that they talked themselves into near-paralysis and an ineffective patchwork of proposals.

As The Tribune's series of articles during the past two weeks has made achingly clear, the Chicago schools are so bad, they are hurting so many thousands of children so terribly, they are jeopardizing the future of the city so much that drastic solutions must be found. It's too late for easy changes, simple answers, painless posturing. It may even be too late to save all of the children the system is grinding down and spitting out without adequate education.

What's necessary first of all are radical changes to wrestle the schools away from the bureaucrats and the unions. The "blob" of the central school system bureaucracy must be exploded, as U.S. Education Secretary William Bennett put it. And the Chicago Teachers Union contract must be dumped. This is major surgery. It will hurt. The recovery period will be shaky. But without it, the schools will not improve.

Several proposals have been pushed in recent months aimed at shifting power away from the bureaucracy and the union. The Education Summit recommends establishing a "local school body" for each school, made up of teacher, parent and community representatives; it would help choose a principal who would have a role in selecting the school's teachers. The state Senate has passed a bill establishing 20 local school districts in Chicago, each with an elected board and power to negotiate a contract with teachers. Other school reform measures are pending.

But none of these reform proposals goes far enough. All would leave the central bureaucracy largely in place while adding a new layer or two. The Chicago Teachers Union, which now whipsaws the Board of Education around at will, would have little trouble perpetuating its control under any of the plans put forth by the Education Summit or in proposed legislation. Local school boards could find it difficult to stay independent of political control, especially since unpaid members would need financial help to be elected.

The quickest, surest way to explode the bureaucratic blob, escape from the self-seeking union and develop schools that succeed for children is to set up a voucher system. That would bring new people into school management, assure local control, empower parents, squeeze out bad schools and put the forces of competition to work for improving education.

But for this to happen, the public must be willing to tolerate a significant interruption in school operation. Strikes have shut down city schools many times in recent years, and in each case the pressure to reopen forced settlements that weakened the system still more. The schools cannot improve unless the people of Chicago stand fast against this union bludgeon. In return, they would be free to make their city a national showcase for excellence in urban education.

The new system would work like this. Parents would be given a voucher for each child, to be used to buy a year's education in the school—public or private—selected by the parents. The availability of the money should stimulate creation of a wide range of new schools under a variety of sponsorships. They would have to be attractive places to pull in enough students to be viable. And they would have to do a good job of teaching to hold the children and stay in business. Because most would be privately run, these schools could choose their own teachers and fire those who turned out to be incompetent. And they could select strong, effective principals empowered to create a good learning environment.

Teachers, as independent professionals, would be hired directly by the schools, which would have to offer salaries, benefits, career opportunities and working conditions attractive enough to get teachers good enough to lure and keep students, just as private and parochial schools do now.

A voucher system would not necessarily mean the end of Chicago's public school system, but it would force the system to be good enough to compete for students with well-managed private enterprises. A new city education authority created by the legislature could reopen the best schools in the system, rehire the best principals and the best teachers. Other school plants could be leased to private school contractors who meet high standards.

To encourage the development of good schools for students who need them most, the vouchers should carry extra reimbursement for those from poor homes, those who can't speak English and those with learning disabilities. The state still could require a core curriculum and monitor the results with standardized tests.

Vouchers also should be available for early learning programs for disadvantaged youngsters at risk of academic failure. Parents of babies and toddlers should get vouchers to pay for visiting teachers who go into homes to help with early mental stimulation and parenting skills, and for neighborhood child-parent centers. Those with preschoolers should have vouchers for nursery schools, Head Start programs, Montessori schools or learning-oriented day care. Investing in early learning is the most effective way to improve the mental abilities of children permanently, to increase success in school and to reduce drop-outs, welfare dependency and crime, as several studies clearly show.

The dollars to buy education will go further under a competitive voucher system. Even so, more tax money will be needed. The Tribune series disclosed that the average suburban school district has $800 more per pupil at its disposal annually than does the Chicago school system. That means city schools would need an extra $336 million a year just to equal the financial resources of the average suburban system.

The state legislature and Gov. Thompson—under court order if necessary—must give Chicago its fair share of state school aid. The current formula cheats city schools out of about $100 million a year because it pretends that only 23 percent of their students are from poor families, when federal census data show that nearly half are poor.

Increases in both the state income tax and the Chicago property tax are essential to providing adequate revenue for city schools.

Together, these steps should produce enough money to fund the vouchers at a level high enough to stimulate the creation of attractive, effective new schools.

A big-scale voucher system is still largely untried, although Minneapolis is phasing one in with apparent early success. Many risks are involved. Many questions are still unanswered. The effects on desegregation, for example, can't be predicted. It's not clear whether elitist schools would drain off the best students and leave the others to stagnate. It might even end the public school system in the nation's third largest city.

But Chicago's school system, with fewer than 13 percent white students, now can provide little more than token desegregation in some schools and none at all in most. The magnet schools and academic academies already draw the best students and leave the others to flounder and fail in neglected neighborhoods where competitive, voucher-supported schools might flourish. And if a voucher system meant the end of Chicago's public school system as The Tribune's series describes it, then it would be a cause for celebration and for national emulation.

About this project

A team of seven Tribune reporters and one photographer examined the Chicago Public Schools for seven months to prepare this series of reports. They interviewed hundreds of officials, teachers, parents and children, spent months inside schools, inspected records and traveled to eight cities that are taking innovative steps to solve the problems of urban schools.

In addition, The Tribune commissioned a poll of Chicagoans' and suburbanites' attitudes toward the schools and conducted a survey of top officials of major employers in a broad range of businesses in the city and suburbs. The newspaper also collected data that made it possible for the first time to make meaningful comparisons of revenue collections and spending between Chicago and suburban districts.

The reporting team consisted of Casey Banas, Bonita Brodt, Merrill Goozner, Jean Latz Griffin, Jack Houston, Michele L. Norris and Patrick Reardon.

In addition, seven other Tribune staff members contributed to the reporting: Andrew Bagnato, R. Bruce Dold, Daniel Egler, Sandy Slater, Karen M. Thomas, James Warren and Owen Youngman.

Ovie Carter was the photographer. The photo editors were Jack Corn, Bill Parker and Steve Stroud.

Graphics editors and artists were Patrick Bergner, Jackie Combs, Martin Fischer, Scott Holingue, Nancy I.Z. Reese, Richard Runnion and Tim Williams. Pages were designed by Stephen Cvengros, Dave Jones, Anton Majeri, James Masek and David Smith.

The project was supervised by Tom Stites, associate managing editor for special projects; Ellen Soeteber, assistant managing editor for metropolitan news, and associate metropolitan editor Barbara Sutton, under the supervision of managing editor F. Richard Ciccone, executive editor Jack Fuller and James D. Squires, editor and executive vice president of The Tribune. Associate metropolitan editor Bill Garrett and assistant metropolitan editor Paul Greenslade assisted in the editing.

The series originally appeared in The Tribune between May 15 and 29, 1988.